Essential Love

Essential Love

Poems About Mothers and Fathers, Daughters and Sons

Edited by Ginny Lowe Connors

Poetworks / Grayson Books

Published by Poetworks / Grayson Books
Post Office Box 270549
West Hartford, CT 06127

Publisher's Cataloging-in-Publication
(Provided by Quality Books, Inc.)

Essential Love : poems about mothers and fathers,
   daughters and sons / edited by Ginny Lowe Connors.
   —1st ed.
   p.   cm.
   Includes index.
   ISBN: 0–9675554–1–8 (hc)
   ISBN: 0–9675554–2–6 (softcover)

   1. Family—Poetry.   2. Parent and child—
Poetry.   3. American poetry—20th century.
I.   Connors, Ginny Lowe.

PS595.F34E77 2000   811' .54080354
                               QB199–1791

Library of Congress Catalog Card Number: 00-90146

CONTENTS

Snapshots

Reaching Out and Letting Go

Transitions

Responsibilities and Expectations

Tenderness

Sickness and Healing

Discoveries

Joy and Pleasure

Anger and Grief

Legacies

SNAPSHOTS

I GO BACK TO MAY 1937

Sharon Olds

I see them standing at the formal gates of their colleges,
I see my father strolling out
under the ochre sandstone arch, the
red tiles glistening like bent
plates of blood behind his head. I
see my mother with a few light books at her hip
standing at the pillar made of tiny bricks with the
wrought-iron gate still open behind her, its
sword-tips black in the May air,
they are about to graduate, they are about to get married,
they are kids, they are dumb, all they know is they are
innocent, they would never hurt anybody.
I want to go up to them and say Stop,
don't do it—she's the wrong woman,
he's the wrong man, you are going to do things
you cannot imagine you would ever do,
you are going to do bad things to children,
you are going to suffer in ways you never heard of,
you are going to want to die. I want to go
up to them there in the late May sunlight and say it,
her hungry pretty blank face turning to me,
her pitiful beautiful untouched body,
his arrogant handsome blind face turning to me,
his pitiful beautiful untouched body,
but I don't do it. I want to live. I
take them up like the male and female
paper dolls and bang them together
at the hips like chips of flint as if to
strike sparks from them, I say
Do what you are going to do, and I will tell about it.

AMNIOCENTESIS

B. A St. Andrews

On this gray steel gurney
with its starched white sheets
she lies as if asleep but she is
wide awake. Washed with

dreams she floats: white boat
on whiter water. Piercing her

abdomen like a needle-nosed gar
a camera dives beneath her

surfaces exploring amniotic seas.
at rest then leaping suddenly

with shifting tides one tiny
orca rides, sending greetings

from the same transducer through
which all meanings start. When

that fetal heart (small and dark
and sweet as a pomegranate seed)

beats "Alive, alive," this tv
monitor is a sacred place

where almost mother lifts almost
child in a watery embrace.

4

THE HOSTS

Peggy Hong

After a day and night of turning
inside out, you slip from between
my blood-stained thighs, gasping, snorting.
Turtle rabbit, not battered and homely
the way newborns are supposed to look,
but red and ripe as an early girl
in August, Boddhisatva with dark hair
spiraling like the rings of a sequoia.

Survive, survive, you intone as you
latch on to my breast. You hold on
to your father's pointer, each knuckle
white. You open one puffy eyelid, and
another, staring us down
with your slate gray eyes.

Then your gaze floats
to the corners where the ceiling
meets the walls. Your jaw
falls slack as you greet someone
over my shoulder. I turn too, wondering
what you see, but catch only
the movement of air.

NEWBORN NIGHT

Andrea Potos

I rock while you suck,
your mouth bound to my breast
like some unbreakable seal.
My lids graze my eyes.
The clock ticks dumbly on.
Already beyond 2 a.m.
and the whole world sleeps
without us. But then,
we drifted from them
long ago, dipping
and swelling in this sea of
exhaustion and need, and I
with no more memory of land
than you.

BABY

DC Berry

The shadows cast by his crib light
made him look like a doll in convict clothes,
sleeping, striped head to toe for life.

I stood there old enough
to be his grandfather, then leaned to kiss
his cheeks, and he wasn't a doll,

but an idol—in fuzzy zebra stripes—
a little God—or referee. I scared
him. When he felt my lips,

he screamed like any lifer would
awakened by Father Time breathing in
his face; his cake eater went wide

open as a siren, but every direction
he'd turn was No Exit.
Screaming like he was a new ambulance,

he'd save us even from ourselves,
this small-time Al Capone
Buddha dressed up like a football

swami. But when
I held him to my chest,
he tried to gum

my hairy gristle of a teat.
Seen one you've seen them all, perhaps
he thought—my whiskerless catfish.

Next thing you know, he thought I was
a doll, as the nipple he chomped
down on like a cigar was clear plastic.

Soon, he had settled down,
snoring like a vacuum cleaner,
sucking the room silent again.

SAVANNA REIGNING

Todd Palmer

Upon her highchair perches our new queen,
And she's incensed. With lips clamped tight,
Her highness now rejects our offerings.
We have such gall assuming she'll eat right,
Approaching her with mush and Enfamil.
She's grown carnivorous with just two teeth.
To curb her cravings as she's fit to kill,
We pile dainty balls of pork and beef
Upon her tray. She snatches at the spoon
As if the one who holds the silverware
Shall reign supreme. Her mom and I will soon
Bow out as suppliants and then prepare
    To watch her, rigged with rows of teeth, attack
    This well-armed world that often bites you back.

WAITING IN THE HALL FOR A SON FIGHTING IN THE LOCKER ROOM

Penelope Deakin

Younger boys are
drifting in and out
muffled sounds deep behind the
closed door.
His own friends
don't appear
even though practice
is long over.
Mothers wait
in the parking lot
suppers growing cold at home.
Finally,
a clutch of sweaty boys
breaks out,
wheels away,
bursts into electric whispers.
He struggles out
last. Tear tracks
on a red face,
hair wet from
who knows what.
Nothing to say
all the way home.

WHILE WE REST

Thom Ward

he cleans his room, sifts
through books, games, puzzles,
Ninja Turtles, colored markers,
burbling silly make-up songs.
Hey Mom! His voice comes
through the wall.
Where'd you put my ascension cord?

I don't know sweetie,
try checking beneath your lamp...
most of her body crumpled into sleep.
He goes back to work,
pushing off the nose cones of his sneaks,
stacking what will fit
on cheap, plastic shelves.

When his reach falls short,
he hops, jumps and throws a book
to the top deck, picks up a matchbox car,
hops, jumps, throws again.
Some things in this life stay put.
Our son is not one of them.
From the start his eyes were on

the attic, the trap door of his mother,
she, listless from the spinal.
It must have been then
he first used his ascension cord,
slick with starshine and mud,
to climb from that world
to this. We cannot keep him
out of trees and forts, from leaping
at banners, door frames, basketball nets.
He stands on counters and chairs,

the lip of our neighbor's picket fence—
Look Dad, it's a cinch—hangs like a clothespin
from the school's monkey bars.
So, in the tangle of his room

there is always the chance
he may stumble upon his lost
ascension cord. A magic string,
a secret rope we have never touched,
but would use if he showed us
how to pitch it over the rafters,
chalk our hands, set our grip,
climb fist after fist into the fabulous air.

THE WINDOW OF MY PARENTS

June Owens

It is late afternoon.
My father comes home,
Stomping through the kitchen door.
He tells us that the hay is in,
Drinks two long glasses of lemonade.
My mother smiles at him.
She unties her apron,
Lets the strings dangle.
They move around each other
As though the air separating them
Is like touch, like conversation.
Something urgent passes between them.
They lead each other, follow each other
To the shiny-floored hall,
Slowly ascend the noisy, narrow stairs,
And curve away beyond my sight.

I am a child and yet I know
They do not go upward
To test the sash weights,
They will not speak
Of carpets that need tacking.
And I know I am expected
To go to the yard and play.
But, because I am a child
I do not know if I
Should rejoice or grieve for them.
So, I keep looking,
Looking upward at their window,
Wondering and, after a while,
Behind me the love-seeking crickets
Take up their songs again.

THE VIOLIN LESSON

Richard Broderick

My ten-year-old and her teacher
stand in a pool of light
which seems right now
to be of their own making,
generated by the gentle sawing
of bows on strings; by the notes
that row stroke after stroke
over a sea of rosin dust;
and then, in the pauses,

by his murmured advice,
her murmured response,
a pianissimo of glowing voices.
In how many ages past
has this scene been re-enacted?
Master and apprentice,
shipwright and journeyman,
making music, laying keels.
With each lesson, I know

She pushes herself further
and further from my shore,
but why would I want to stop her?
Her teacher taps the stand.
She brings the violin up
to her chin, her arms raised
as if she were breasting a swell,
a small vessel setting forth
beneath a spar of sound.

HAVING

Ginny Lowe Connors

Your cousins have so much more
than you, computers, game
systems, vacation trips, while you,
you have not even a father
to speak of, but still
here you are, the last of the sun
lighting up your hair, as evening breathes gold
into the sky, the air warm, scented with hay,
whispering stay
stay just a little longer in this place.
You reach for more berries, lick fingers, reach again
for more from the mulberry tree
which seems to hold all of your wishes.
All around, the ground is blotchy with berries,
mottled like your own fair skin when you are fevered
with illness, anger or dream.
Hands and mouth stained purple, you turn to me smiling,
your eyes embers that glow and glow,
the evening's first stars.
Now swallows are swooping like grace
through the dusk and I think,
without any reason at all,
that for once you have everything in the world
you could want
and so do I.

MY SON, WHO CAN'T SIT STILL

Ginny Lowe Connors

Picasso looked at the women he painted
with many eyes; he saw complexity, and took in
the hopeful glance at dawn, a hunger
at noon, never a stillness or a single perspective,
but the shift and movement humanity shares with sunlight
rippling across a lake. And so I see my son,
the fifteen year old boy before me,
rearranging beans on a yellow plate,
speaking earnestly about hypocrisy one moment, laughing
moments later, at everyone who assumes control.
The child of three is before me too, asking countless questions,
even as he moves the toothbrush up and down,
even as he spits.
I see him coasting down the driveway
on a spotted plastic pony; he feels the sweet delight
of trouble, coasts right into it without a backward glance.
Pouring two mugs of tea, I peer through the steam and see
the man he will become, the restless perplexity, and the pain
too, carried with him, the way a river carries water.
With his eyes closed, he will hold what is pleasing in the palm
of his hand and he will pay for that.
My son swallows and I watch something sharp
slide up and down his throat. I look at him hard and see
he is all angles. His knuckles are chapped
and his fingers are constantly drumming. I place my hand
over his to still the hurried beat of his life,
but, he complains, he is just waiting for something to happen.
He looks at his life and sees a still life, objects
slowly accepting dust; I peer at him through a kaleidoscope;
so many designs are there, changing, rearranging, falling into place.
My son's eyes are the dark blue of evening
just before stars appear
and he is often searching for that calm, that distant light.

Picasso could paint his energy and his waiting,
the tension held within like that of an egg
about to hatch, but if he painted Adam, my son
would gaze at that strange phantom, as if at something
he'd met once in a dream, shake his head and wonder
what it was he recognized.

THE DAY AFTER
MY SON'S BIRTHDAY

Sondra Zeidenstein

What is on my mind
is not his birth
or babyhood—
compact, wide-bellied, hungry boy
suctioning Libby's pureed lamb
off a silver-plated spoon
offered again and again
until, between one eagerly-lipped offering
and the next,
he is finished and nothing,
no enticing tickle of his lower lip,
no smile or mother's coo
can pry his set lips open.
What's on my mind
is not his untold life
on an old wooden sailboat
plagued with rot
waiting out a season of hurricanes
stuck on the shoals of a life
drink is wrecking.
This poem,
unlike the ones I've written
on other birthdays,
will be short, not the ten-page spill
of longing to have the perfect infant
in my arms again.
This poem welcomes
the chunky, beak-nosed, burnt-skinned, red-eyed man,

lips tight as the clasp
of an old-fashioned satchel,
sullen tilt of his pelted head,
my son at forty.
This poem is grateful for the son I have,
for the eyes to see him.

ADMIRING MY FATHER

Thomas R. Smith

I was at an age when everything he did
fascinated me, was by definition admirable.
I'd have grabbed the cigar from between his teeth
if he'd let me; I insisted on pressing the purring
head of the razor on my cheek. Half-
approving, he'd hand over his men's magazines—
Cavalier or *Argosy*—missing certain glossy pages.

He's gone now, though luckily my mother
snapped him slouched on the davenport
holding me astraddle his waist. I lean into
his face, no more than two inches separating us,
tiny hands gripping his jaw. My expression
is enthusiasm for everything about him—
his look says he knows it's the best I'll ever

give him. When at certain unsuspecting
moments life washes up to my feet something
he preferred—an ice cream flavor or a song—
in the absence of sharp memory I think
of that photo and of those times when I rode
high and happy, the ropes secure,
the wind in my sails, and he was the future

I steered toward, gladly. Now, unsure
whether I've reached his shore—though
his resemblance grows on me year by year—
I feel the old antagonisms drop away
from when the midnight sun of my generation
rose and I threw him away in pieces,
and am flooded again with the power of loving him.

MY FATHER'S PICTURE ON THE COVER OF A BUFFALO BISON'S HOCKEY PROGRAM FOR 1934

Peter Desy

Booze took him from me
when I was too young
to understand, before his real death
in 1979. In this picture
he is about 25. The caption reads
"Speedy Desy, A Rising Star."
I remember when I was small
he passed the puck to me
on the ice rink in the park.
I was pumping wildly, reaching
for his pass. It hit my stick
perfectly, and I've never felt so whole
as then — skating fast on the flat earth,
the wind at our backs, sailing
off the edge at full speed,
never landing, my arms around
his neck, the big stars
everywhere, all around us.

AFTER MY STEPFATHER'S DEATH

Wesley McNair

Again it is the moment when I left home
for good, and my mother is sitting quietly
in the front seat while my stepfather pulls me
and my suitcase out of the car and begins
hurling my clothes, though now
I notice for the first time how the wind
unfolds my white shirt and puts its slow
arm in the sleeve of my blue shirt and lifts them
all into the air above our heads so beautifully
I want to shout at him to stop and look up
at what he has made, but of course when I turn
to him, a small man, bitter even this young
that the world will not go his way, my stepfather
still moves in his terrible anger, closing the trunk,
and closing himself into the car as hard as he can,
and speeding away into the last years of his life.

TO MY FATHER, DYING IN A SUPERMARKET

Wesley McNair

At first it is difficult
to see you
are dropping dead—

you seem lost
in thought, adjusting your tie
as if to rehearse

some imaginary speech
though of course beginning
to fall,

your mouth opening wider
than I have ever seen
a mouth,

your hands deep
in your shirt,
going down

into the cheeses, making the sound
that is not
my name,

that explains nothing
over and over,
going away

into your hands
into your face,
leaving this great body

on its knees
the father
of my body

which holds me
in this world,
watching you go

on falling
through the musak,
making the sound

that is not my name,
that will never
explain anything, oh father,

stranger, all dressed up
and deserting me
for the last time.

THE WINDOW, AUTUMN

William Reichard

Outside, she rakes maple leaves into loose piles, stakes burlap and wire
around roses rarely coaxed to bloom. From inside, I watch my mother
through old windows, and she is changed by the bend of the pane.

Old glass, slow as continents, drifts down over years,
pools at the bottom of the sill and spreads the world out in a new spectrum.
Old glass, viscous as memory, runs, unseen.

She moves on. The leaves sit in ordered mounds until the wind comes;
she begins to prune the hedges, collects grass at the base of the fence.
The summer starts to push away in the promise of a brittle breeze and

she cleans. She cleans. Outside, my mother is transformed,
a woman woven into the trees, her hands, her face warped
and spread into the branches, a body bent and blending

across the lawn. Now, she knows a world without children,
lives in a place I've never seen. She stoops over, throws a stone
into the deep ditch, snaps down brown milkweed.

BLOODROOT

Simone Poirier-Bures

When they held her up,
newly emerged,
the cold, strange air
hitting her skin, she flung out
arms, legs, hands and feet grasping
flexing, red and angry like some crustacean
dragged up from the bottom of the sea.

She gasped and flailed while they washed her,
The air! The light!
raging at this forced
displacement, that terrible journey for this
terrible journey's end.

When they placed her on her mother's belly,
covered her loosely, you could see
an instant change in her. In that cave
of dark warmth, she almost smiled,
riding the waves of mother-breath,
the thudding, watery heartbeat.
Home again.

Her mother, lifting the blanket's edge: *Oh
baby!* A whoosh of breath. The knot
between them sudden, electric.

Watching this on the videotape you made
I feel my own womb quicken. Twenty-three years
ago, you on my belly. That fierce
joining. The same thick

bloodroot
extending, now, to her.

BIRTHDAY CELEBRATION, CARL'S CHOP HOUSE, DETROIT

Peter Desy

The waiters there wear tuxedos and have hushed
attitudes, as if feeding
were a formal affair, something
we do once a year that needs exactitude and
supervision. August 21, the table formally
arranged, my mother at the head.
"I'm eighty today," she announces
and we clap and clank our glasses
with our knives.

                          She looks so small
cutting her thick lamb chops—the thin
architecture of her hands showing through
paper skin—excising the meat neatly,
chewing, satisfying desire, being there,
wholly, with the family busy with their meat,
and the silverware tinkling and flashing
in the artificial light. Outside, dark now,
and everything moving now—stars, moon, clouds,
wind and cars. We go single file toward
the door, finished with the sharp, curved bones
of animals left on our plates. We almost
feel the earth move as we step into
the night, the leaves spangled silver
as the light takes them and moves on.

MY MOTHER WHO CAN'T

Lyn Lifshin

see my face clear enough
to know me in Macy's
until she hears my
voice wants to go
out in trees, look
for the comet.
She sighs that she
used to be able to
jump up from a yoga
position, now has to
catch her breath. She
wants to learn to
disco, says when
she wanted to dance
they wouldn't let her
still she danced on bare
toes as if her feet were
in Pointe shoes. The
comet, she says like a
child dreaming of
marzipan, we could
go out in the trees,
look up from that
brightness lashing us
with light that won't
be here again for
200 years, as she moves
by touching the
scarred red wood
slowly up stairs she
used to take three
at a time.

DRIVING HOME TO SEE THE FOLKS

Anthony Sobin

Asleep at the wheel nearly
dead I think
and feeling nothing
but the dark eyes of the Wyoming antelope
on my skin—watching me pass—a small animal
growling down the highway
with both eyes aglow.

To keep awake
I push my head out the window
as into a guillotine
the black wind and sleet
slipping under each eyelid
like a child's thin silver spoon.

Looking back into the car
through the ice and tears
I do not recognize that body sleeping there.
I no longer know that leg pressed hard
to the gas, that blue coat or wool scarf or
that hand reaching out to the wheel.

Folks, you know I am doing my best—
pushing hard toward you
through this winter sky
but reduced to this—

just this head out a window
streaming through space like a bearded rock,
a hunk of pocked iron with melting eyes.

The trail of fiery mist
growing out from the back of my head
stretches now for miles across the night.

The odds, I know, are a thousand to one
in favor of my burning up before touching earth

but if somehow I do make it home
smashing across the farmyard
and lighting up the sky

I will throw a red glow across the barn's silver roof
and crash into the rough wood of your back door
smaller than a grain of sand
making its one childlike knock.

The porch light will hesitate,
then snap on, as it always does
when a car comes up the lane
late at night.

The two sleepy old faces
will come to the door
in their long soft robes—
will stand there bewildered
rubbing their eyes
looking around and wondering
who it was at their door

no sooner come than gone

a cinder in the eye.

EASTER SUNDAY, 1955

Elizabeth Spires

*Why should anything go wrong in our bodies? Why should we not
be all beautiful? Why should there be decay?—why death?—and,
oh, why damnation?*

—Anthony Trollope, in a letter

What were we? What have we become?
Light fills the picture, the rising sun,
the three of us advancing, dreamlike,
up the steps of my grandparents' house on Oak Street.
My mother and father, still young, swing me
lightly up the steps, as if I weighed nothing.
From the shadows, my brother and sister watch,
wanting their turn, years away from being born.
Now my aunts and uncles and cousins
gather on the shaded porch of generation,
big enough for everyone. No one has died yet.
No vows have been broken. No words spoken
that can never be taken back, never forgotten.
I have a basket of eggs my mother and I dyed yesterday.
I ask my grandmother to choose one, just one,
and she takes me up—O hold me close!—
her cancer not yet diagnosed. I bury my face
in soft flesh, the soft folds of her Easter dress,
breathing her in, wanting to stay forever where I am.
Her death will be long and slow, she will beg
to be let go, and I will find myself, too quickly,
in the here-and-now moment of her fortieth year.
It's spring again. Easter. Now my daughter steps
into the light, her basket of eggs bright, so bright.
One, choose one, I hear her say, her face upturned
to mine, innocent of outcome. Beautiful child,
how thoughtlessly we enter the world!
How free we are, how bound, put here in love's name
—death's too—to be happy if we can.

REACHING OUT AND
LETTING GO

I SIT, HYPNOTIZED BY STORM

Liz Abrams-Morley

Or by wind, mostly and the cat,
distracted, places his purple fur
mouse under

the couch, over
and over. I am drawn to metal
ping of hail bits blown against cold

windows knowing, against my better
judgment I must place in my neighbor's car
my purple snow—

suited son, most
precious and animated, dying,
he tells me, to witness the game:

Penn versus Princeton. He will
replay the way each balls rims one
perfect circle

and drops
through net the way wet sleet
swishes, graying red brick homes

to tombstones. *Don't sue, Promise
you won't sue,* my neighbor's saying
half laugh,

half strain,
my son buckling hurriedly as she's
pulling away. Through snow veil

I watch and watch the dot van
like the cat, staring where his toy
once was

or at a dark
under the sofa he must believe
has devoured it, chain and all.

Where's Jesse? I used to call
as over and over my son covered
round brown eyes

with fat fists
as if he believed this small act
tantamount to his disappearance.

Where's Jesse? I'd ask and listen
for the laugh, watch the brown eyes,
shivering, returned.

WORRYWART

Victor M. Depta

A frozen winter, I hate it
snow, ice storm, more snow
though the kids are in heaven
angels on the ground, snowballs, snowmen
and sled riding past dark.

I trudge to the hill to drag her home
but no, she needs a push, just one more
and one more, and one more.
I sigh, glance at the stars, and shove.

As she drops away I worry.
It's so dark down there
she goes so fast, out of my hands
so unseen in the white-dark, bluing-dark
her yells so distant.

I shudder and look at the stars.
God, I think, how literary, how symbolic
but, as a matter of fact, the night was starry
brilliant-hard, dark-glittering
and she slid away from me, many times.

NATURAL BUOYANCY

Judith Strasser

You were two months old
when we stood in the pool at the "Y,"
hip-deep in chlorine-heavy water
warm as a mother's womb. We pushed
you through the ripples
coaxing, "Swim to Daddy," "Swim
to Mommy," trusting baby fat
and reflex to keep you afloat
and breathing properly.

Just as, when the stewardess
leads you down the jetway,
your backpack slung
over one shoulder, sporty (or
is it cool?), I picture you,
not as a shuttlecock, hurtling
toward your father through thin air
and turbulence, but more like
a kestrel, soaring, held aloft
by thermals and your natural buoyancy.

THE ARTIST'S WAY

Jane Butkin Roth

Picture this:
she, who has no memory of
happy family life,
no childhood without
forced divisions of loyalty,

takes her simple tools—a sketch pad,
a palette of color,
transforms her "tabula rasa,"

her picture always has a sun with
a large friendly face, a man and wife,
standing tall and smiling, holding hands
                    holding children's
hands on a hill that's
always green that
always grows bright
flowers, and

when she's finished,
her soft eight-year old
eyes look up
at some grown-up
for approval,

unaware of the message she paints,
the lessons she teaches through her picture
which tells us to
believe again, as she believes

all things are possible
even this:
a family
enduring.

WHAT MY MOTHER BELIEVED

Laura Stearns

She believed he would return,
her father's spirit a white tendril
traveling the length of our house.
The enchanted child she would follow him,
finally able to call back all the lost summers.
They would eat from a can of sardines,
as they had once during the Depression,
then drive to the farm at Outlook
to visit the aunts and uncles still playing rummy
in the dark kitchen. But when he did return,
standing in the doorway
dressed in his best suit,
his hat tipped as he wavered between worlds,
all she did was nod in recognition,
perhaps thinking "so this is the sadness
that all of my grief belongs to."
Who am I to say what's real
and what's imagination, the heart's longing for witness.
I too want to believe that the dead don't leave,
like old hymns they keep returning,
waiting for someone to recognize their beauty and sing.

IF YOU HAVE NEVER
SEEN A HORSE

Siv Cedering

Say that you've never seen a horse
grazing in a field
or galloping at the edge of the sea,
that you have never sat high on the back
of a mare, or melted into her motion,
that you have never felt
the soft velvet of a muzzle
looking for something
in your hand,
yet you have heard hooves
and awakened to a feeling of horses.
However fast and far
you speed through cities
or out into space
on monorail trains or rockets,
the horses will come
to graze quietly in your dream
and nuzzle you awake
at dawn.

Say that you have not seen your father
for years, or ever,
that he has not taught you baseball
or bought you a bat, or a cap,
that he has not carried you on his shoulders
or paced the floor of the room
where you lay ill,
that as far as you know, he has never
stood in the dark, watching you sleeping,
or come to your rescue
in the school yard.
Yet he will enter your room, some night.

You will sense his presence
and fall asleep,
knowing he will stay there,
waiting for you to rescue him
from forgetfulness
and keep him safe
in the dark.

WHEN THE CALL CAME

Norbert Krapf

When the call came
I was about to cut the grass
for the first time. Wild
onion and dandelion were
spouting across the lawn.
Sheaths of lily of the valley
bearing round green bells
were surrounding the lilac.

When the call came
the yellow marsh marigolds
were rising like the sun
against a boulder in
the flower bed. Bees
buzzed around bunches
of purple grape hyacinth.
The operator said, *I have
a collect call from Columbia.
Do you accept the charges?*
I replied, *Yes. I accept.*

When the call came
the leathery leaves
of bloodroot along the ledge
of the stone wall were
wrapped around stalks
like green sheets on which
white petals lay. Beside
the fishpond the fronds
of maidenhair fern were
unfurling in the sun.
A voice with a Spanish
accent spoke in my ear,

This is a social worker. We
have a baby girl born eight
days ago. Will you accept her?

When the call came
the white blossoms
of the wild cherry at the edge
of the woods were fluttering
on black boughs. The tips
of Japanese irises were
pushing through the soil.
Specks of bibb lettuce
lay like green confetti
on the upper level of
the rock garden. *Yes, we*
accept her, I said, *Yes.*

ADOPTION

Crystal Williams

My name, you whispered, let fly
from your lips, exhaled and I was not a baby—
of ringlets and milky brown eyes—but winged
and flying from your arms.
Leaving what, a hole?
an indentation on the blanket?

At four days old, light brown and borrowed,
like sugar from a neighbor,
they opened their door and drew me

in. Wrapped their arms around
the smile Momma says has always been
larger than the joelouis arena and taught me
to walk, my wings becoming shoes
and Easter bonnets and pink Huffies.

Woman, do your arms
get cold and concave with the
coming of September 26th?
What of your Alabama husband
and your mother who looked
Native, her hair blue black straight? Did
they see the Hale-Bopp and think of me?
And did your other six children,
their brown eyes longing, look
just over your shoulder to
the clear sky? Have they asked my name?
Surely they have asked my name...

TO MY BOY, ASLEEP

Gianna Russo

Bedded down on bare floor,
a little cowboy
uncertain of the new bunk
stretching dark as a tree and moss-high,
you are freshly four
and already snoring
like a bullfrog.

Your camp is all boy,
ringed with bow and arrow,
cap-gun, Robin Hood hat, pirate sword.
These like lucky charms surround you
bright as birthstones with you
shining from the center of a dream.
Before ever I held you
I dreamed you.

Now I'm drawn to this shadowed door
to watch you sleep,
a dormant cyclone.
I feel too soon here
the gentle pull
like a kite straining in my hand,
how already you are leaving,
your infancy lost as dates
left out of the baby book.
Little arrow,
you are flying
and already there are days
when your look is a foreign climate,
my anger unspeakable as a curse.
Such days I search for good
and afterwards

my hands smooth your hair,
smooth the thunder from your face
in a prayer
that the lessons you are bringing
I can accept.
Perhaps that is the only test.

Tonight your doorway
holds me like a spell
with the crickets' mantra
soft at the window,
the night air sweet as a blessing.
The woodsprites are setting the earthworms turning
but I myself can't turn away,
though your father sighs into his pillows,
for your little chest rises like bread,
your room is full
and awake with wishes.

THE FAR COUNTRY

Richard Hague

A sleeping child gives me the impression of a traveler in a far country

—Emerson, *Journals*

For an hour he has called and called for me,
fighting sleep.
I have answered with lullabies and stories.
Now, dozing in my arms,
he falls utterly away,
spirited off by an eyeless stranger
to a place of waves and yellow sky.
To whom do I give him in sleep?
Soon, distant and adrift,
he becomes a memory
whose name I cannot pronounce,
some saint
for whom there is no body,
mostly light and air.

Every night I send him hopelessly off,
then, repentant, want to
bring him back
from his terrible exile,
the nightmares he cannot even name.
I want my voice to reach him where he is,
lapsed into a beauty
as appalling as death's.

But I am silenced, helpless.
A far sea's rhythmic surge
overtakes his breathing:
in his boat of skin
he voyages his own dark way,
wandering where he must,
coming back only if he can.

ON MORGAN STREET

Anne McCrady

A black dog follows you down
The sidewalk as if you have called
Him, as if you could.
Not yet to the age of speech,
Your rendition of his species,
Like all our other attempts
At words, comes out in double
Syllabled drops of simple sounds:
Ga-ga, Bye-bye, No-no,
Dots and dashes only those
Who love you understand.
Ahead of you, the trees lean in
To lend their frame to the evening
Picture of a summer stroll,
Of the edges of manhood:
Your tiny wobbles alongside
Mr. Campbell's swaying steps.
He is seventy today, and your gift
To him is to leave me here
Watching you go
Walking around the block with him:
Your first time away from home
For a guy's night out!
The ragged grass along the concrete
Squares makes the path
Seem rural and rustic, somehow safe.
I imagine other routes
You will choose,
Other backs I will face.
Just before you turn the corner
And disappear out of sight,
I see you look up at Mr. Campbell

In a love subtracted
From the focused devotion you have had

For me. May I someday find
A note from you attached
To such a gift.

CAT'S CRADLE

Carol Wade Lundberg

Each time we leave, after
        a thousand hugs and kisses,
a thousand schemes to make us stay
and promises to come back soon
she must run quickly, before
her mother calls her back, to find
us some small gift: a ribbon,
a piece of colored paper, a pink
plastic brush from her Barbie collection—

pressing them into our hands as if
we must carry some part of her home;
already she has learned the uncertainty
of the world, thinks with five-year-old
logic to hedge her bets, believing
the deities would not call us away
with accounts of giving and receiving
so incomplete. I marvel at her

open bribery, her willingness to
reveal the urgencies of love without
camouflage of nonchalance, to lay
bare how much she wants us, how
greedily she plots to keep us in her
life, leaving nothing unspoken,
nothing to chance—neither our good
intentions or their ripening. We glow

like Roman candles at such shameless
caring, drive home hoarding our secret
joy, unable to match her undressed love.
But next week she will start school,
will find a world of small energies like

her own, will warm herself with their
sameness and their mystery, will learn
to her salvation and delight faces
of love outside the kinship circle,

and I wonder how long it will be
before we leave unnoticed while she
chatters on the phone, how long
before those visits when I press into
her hands a box of homemade cookies,
the antique doll she used to play with,
an old photo of the two of us when
she was three, anything I can think of
to hold her in my life.

WHAT IS SUPPOSED TO HAPPEN

Naomi Shihab Nye

When you were small,
we watched you sleeping,
waves of breath
filling your chest.
Sometimes we hid behind
the wall of baby, soft cradle
of baby needs.
I loved carrying you between
my own body and the world.

Now you are sharpening pencils,
entering the forest of
lunch boxes, little desks.
People I never saw before
call out your name
and you wave.

The loss I feel,
this shrinking,
as your field of roses
grows and grows...

Now I understand history.
Now I understand my mother's
ancient eyes.

SCHOOLWARD

Mark Defoe

I

It's a morning with fall glinting
On the leaves, the trees laced with birds
As if pure song could make summer last.

I walk my children one last time
To their first day of school. Next year
They'll join that rowdy tribe that stuffs
And disgorges from the rumbling bellies
Of the great rock-n-rollin orange buses.

Now they bring me between them, like some oaf
Held back ten grades. They talk around me
In school girl code, voices flirting with joy,
But careful—they are old hands now. They glide,
Combed and tucked in their annual newness.
They allow me to hold their cool hands,
At least until we near the school yard.

II

We parents find it hard to meet this way,
Caught in our tenderness. A lady
In pink churns by, two husky boys
Like outriggers. Her lips are set,
Hands knotted to her children's hands.

III

Each at her door, we part with some small touch.
I give them over to imperfect strangers,
No less unwise than I, to be molded
Into a someone neither I
Nor teacher can quite call our own.

IV

As I pass a class, I pause. A woman
Stands among them. Her lips command.
From the rows, slender arms sprout up,
Swaying in the warmth of her smile.

V

Homebound, peace has come. Even the jays
Have stopped quibbling. My life spreads
Before me—banal and stupid.

Suddenly, I'm that boy again,
That shy boy who loves his teacher.
Raise your hand, a voice says. Tell her.
You know it. Tell her. You know the answer.

REARVIEW MIRROR

John M. Roderick

There is always pain driving away
That is heightened by the parting glance
In the rearview mirror of my car.

There, miniaturized against the road ahead
Is the image of a boy running along the roadside
Waving constantly to the father leaving again,
A small image of a small boy
That looms larger with each departure.

I have watched a boy grow up in that mirror,
Watched wisps of blond hair
Grow coarser and darker
And watched fleshy legs in short pants
Grow longer and slender,
But still they run after my car,
And always the face remains the same,
And the eyes that peer back at me
Through the rearview mirror...
Burn into my heart.

AT THE CROSSROADS

Mary Scott

Tonight I buy my son a mountain bike.
Independent of his father
we pick a bicycle from a rack of wheels.
It's already assembled and has eighteen speeds,
more than an eleven-year-old needs.

George walks the bike out to the car but refuses
to let me carry it home in the trunk. He says
the frame will get nicked where the latch hits it.
I don't argue much, remembering how my ex-husband
gouged the cabinet on my new sewing machine
removing it from the van and how the scratch ruined
my pleasure every time I sewed.

It's dark now but my son begs to ride home,
three miles from the shopping center.
I can't let him venture out alone like that,
not yet. We compromise. I accompany him,
monitor his progress along the route.
He takes off and I follow, track him like radar.
No parking allowed on the main street, so I forge ahead,
stop at parking lots and side streets to wait.

He takes longer than I think he should.
I know his father wouldn't approve,
would have hoisted the bike into the trunk and hauled it home,
made him wait another day to try his wheels.
I'd be home now instead of standing on an isolated corner
peering down a dark corridor of trees for my son to emerge.
It's always been this way, me just ahead watching
my child clambering after, searching for me like a landmark.

At each junction he appears, weary and relieved.
Every day he pedals farther away from me
and I sense the time approaching
when he won't need me to navigate the night with him
like two bats squeaky as hinges at twilight
but tonight he still looks for me at every intersection.
Just as much, I need to measure how much distance
I must put between us in order to stay this close.

VISITATION RITES

Jack Myers

My gentle son is performing tricks for me on his bicycle.
He's fourteen and has just cracked open the storm door
to manhood with his gently lowered voice shredding
into shadows until he's surrounded by the calls of
ten young girls whose smooth brown skin calls out, "We're alone."

It will not be long before he masters standing still
on one wheel, elegant jumps over obstacles, riding
upside down and backwards until he will have made
of danger a pretty colored bird to delight him,
sending it away, calling it home, calling it home
as it sails and grows larger, darkens and adds weight.

I watch how well he has done without me all these years,
me with my iron sled of guilt, my cooked-out piles of
worry smoldering. I have been his only model, he says,
and shares with me what a typical day of winning is like.
I sit on a little hill watching my son show off his
light dominion over gravity, knowing in the next few minutes

I will leave him again for another year, and again our lives
will pull apart and heal over like bubbles separating in two.
This is how he says good-bye—without speech or reasons or
the long looking after that I have honed through time—
just in a flash in the sun he's suddenly perfected, and I'm gone.

ROOM FOR SONG

Mary Makofske

Lately my sons are rapt
in rooms bristling with warnings—
Keep Out! No Trespassing.
This Means YOU!
I trespass, by the cracks
closed doors can give
into their lives. Inside,
footfalls, a rustling.

No calculating how far
they have walked
between the windows and the white
iron beds their bodies now
can take measure of.
Under my feet the floor begins to pulse
with music they inhabit like a room,
locked, as these old doors won't lock.

After their baths, I enter the steam
they've left, breathe deeply, gather
towels like shed skins.
As in the rain forest after
a storm, one by one
the birds pick up their songs.

I WISH I COULD HOLD YOU
AS TREES HOLD THEIR LEAVES

Ginny Lowe Connors

You shy from my touch, turn toward the door.
Glancing back, you raise up the palms
of your hands, exasperated.
Grownups are dense, cannot hear
your music, cannot feel the light rising up
through your body, lifting you right off the ground.

Daughter, I wish I could hold you as trees
hold their leaves, green, lovely
in May's new-washed light,
which we are thankful for.
As you hesitate, scents
of spring drift around you: cut grass,
damp soil pushed aside by green things opening up.

The delicate palms of your hands reach out
catching sunlight, cloud shadows, trembling
slightly in evening's chilly air.
Tiny drops of rain are falling now
into the cups of young leaves.
Something close to understanding
flies between us. I blink
and once again, you're gone.

UNNESTING

Mary Lee McNeal

With indelible ink
I write the name I gave you
on each towel and sheet
before I fold and place them
in this trunk—
        as if I could mark you
any longer as mine!
        as if we both didn't know
you're a woman now, bound
        to name yourself:
                separate

I am remembering
the days spent washing, folding
tiny nightgowns and blankets,
scrubbing the places you'd lie,
trying to imagine you,
        a stranger about to burst
        from my own belly,
grateful to find a name for
unfamiliar domesticity:
             nesting instinct

Now, eighteen years later
I'm unable to name
these strangely soothing
preparations to send you away.
What to call this
pulling apart of the nest?
        this plucking out
of the feathers and sticks
which have bound us?

This has no name, my
daughter, this instinct
         to help you leave,
this terrible urge to
         push you out.

FOR MEG, LEAVING HOME

Netta Gillespie

Lights on everywhere, except where I am sitting
Writing this first letter since you left,
Knowing that what I write, I will not send—
That one comes later, full of cheerful news;
This is the one I have to write to me.

Once you were all promise, flower in the bud,
Sitting like Buddha on your yellow rug,
Catching the sun's motes with your fingers,
Your thoughts mysterious, wordless; and I felt
Nothing could come between you and the light.

But now I know first child has more to break
Than barriers of blood and bone; the soul's old pain,
The dark confusions of the blood, remain;
And all that karmic legacy broods still
Over the sunrise of your going forth.

Today I cleared your room of those old treasures
You could not bear to put away yourself:
Flotsam of empty bottles, unburned candles,
Paper flowers faded from the sun,
Buckles, yellow stockings, birthday cards;

And when I had finished the room stood stripped of your presence
Except for one orange flower and a Van Gogh print;
I felt like a nurse with an antiseptic bottle
Tidying up after death, removing all traces,
Putting what's left behind in boxes;

And my throat was thick with the things I could never say,
Or even if I had, you could not have listened to;
And you are sent out on that same exhausting journey
Through wrong choices, false love. Yet for love's sake
I hurl you into the universe, and pray.

FROM A PHONE BOOTH

Margaret Diorio

Friday night supper over, the phone rings.
Fatigue honing her thin voice, my daughter
calling from a great distance from a phone booth
in a girls' dormitory thanks me.

Her thermal underwear, vitamins, my poem
arrived. Mornings the wind-chill index is forty
below. Insomnia, Plato. Words reaching out
in new concerns enter the blank pages

of her life. Snow falls. All roads are blocked.
It is 1978, and she, a freshman, seeks answers.
I utter directions for her safekeeping.
Silence comes back across the mountains

like a freight of steeples. Eyes and lips
have not changed. The loss of golden glow
and evening teas is a fledgling flying between us.
She is talking common sense; tension and stamina mix.

The world she describes is eighteen, snowy white, merciless.
She is in love. She, that white bloom I put out in December.

TO AN ONLY DAUGHTER

Tom Hansen

So today
we give you away;
your other father, the one
who took you in
when he married your mother;
and I,
your natural father,
who so unnaturally
let you go—
when it was too
late to hold on.

Yet now we two
old fathers embrace.
We hold in our arms the emptiness
of those who learn
too late that they
too soon release
what, after all,
was never really theirs to call
their own.
And so you
move on.

NOW DAUGHTER

Sondra Zeidenstein

Now daughter, when we sit across from each other,
necks thrust forward, talking about your work,
how you midwife babies into the world
and you skim with two fingers
your soft dry lips as you talk,
or trace a sensitive fingertip around your chin,
I remember how I stroked your cheek,
its fine red veins,
as you sucked the nipple of your bottle.
God! how long you would take sucking
with mild, half-interested puckers—
an hour almost for three ounces.
I think you didn't have an appetite
for spending your days in my silences,
my other-mindedness,
when I wasn't fitting you into your pink nylon snowsuit,
tucking you deep in the shadow of the carriage,
putting you down in playpen, high chair, sandbox.
I think you wanted to hold me there,
make me look from the blue and white dance of television
to the small pink birth stains
fading between your eyebrows.
I wanted to sleep, to burrow into my darkness.
I gave you morning nap, afternoon nap, put you to sleep
at six. My dog—russet at the corner of my eye—
let my faint interest be enough, but you made me
watch your clear eyes doze up under your lids,
made me touch your cheek, tickle the small fat sole
of your foot, flick it with thumb and middle finger
until your body startled
and your lazy mouth remembered.
You set yourself against my darkness,
spun my like a thread from my knotted spirit.
You held me to the world.

TO MY DAUGHTERS

MaryLee McNeal

Through rain, into the library,
too laden to use an umbrella,
I hug a stack of books under my coat.

Even under shelter of eaves I press
books close to my body, hands clasped
under their weight, a middle-aged woman

waddling through stacks, holding books
like unborn babies, remembering how
I held myself when I was pregnant,

Fingers interlaced under my belly
in just this way, as if I could keep my
daughters from dropping into this world.

I imagine the words in books the same way
I imagined the bones of my daughters, through
all the skin and the waters, the blood between us.

My daughters, I have carried and borne you.
I have held you so tightly I might have
broken all of us. But look!

We have each survived, separate and whole.
I have opened my arms now, and we are free.
Return to me when you will, if you will.

I turn back to myself.
I am pregnant again.
I am pregnant with desire for these books.

ANNUAL VISIT

Harold Black

I.

On Sunday, my father Abraham
packed us in his Chevrolet, drove us
to a picnic on Belle Isle.

Sun glistened on the river.
We watched ore boats slipping by,
shattering the stillness with their whistles.

We munched on Kosher hot dogs,
drank Vernor's ginger ale,
joked in broken English.

Years have passed. Now I drive
the Pennsylvania Turnpike
past trucks, steeples and tiny houses.

Grandma Moses scenes unfold,
I see nothing, remember only
Sunday picnics on Belle Isle.

I ring a bell, see my shriveled father.
I sweep him up,
His skinny arms around my neck.

II.

Here, in this house of memories,
I watch you and your friends
play cards on Sunday nights,
raise money, write letters
for Jews in Poland. One day
no answers come.

One by one they dwindle,
until there are not enough
to sit around a table
playing cards.

You tell me stories
of an empty synagogue,
where rain drips
on a warped floor.
My father, as I leave,
you press your face
against the window.
Your eyes follow my car.

You will sit there
playing solitaire
and grow so thin,
you'll drift away
in the morning wind.

MY FATHER'S NECKTIES

Maxine Kumin

Last night my color-blind chain-smoking father
who has been dead for fourteen years
stepped up out of a basement tie shop
downtown and did not recognize me.

The number he was wearing was as terrible
as any from my girlhood, a time of
ugly ties and acrimony: six or seven
blue lightning bolts outlined in yellow.

Although this was my home town it was tacky
and unfamiliar, it was Rabat or Gibraltar
Daddy smoking his habitual
square-in-the-mouth cigarette and coughing
ashes down the lightning jags. He was
my age exactly, it was wordless, a window
opening on an interior we both knew
where we had loved each other, keeping it quiet.

Why do I wait years and years to dream this outcome?
My brothers, in whose dreams he must as surely
turn up wearing rep ties or polka dots clumsily
knotted, do not speak of their encounters.

When we die, all four of us, in
whatever sequence, the designs
will fall off like face masks
and the rayon ravel from this hazy version
of a man who wore hard colors recklessly
and hid out in the foreign
bargain basements of his feelings.

TRANSITIONS

WOMB

Corrine De Winter

In my womb a separate life
quivers, locked in
its cocoon, the void
black eyes unable to tune in.
The lungs no bigger than thumbnails
expand and fall ceaselessly
in the bloody undertow.

My questions echo
in stark white sterile rooms.
Do soundwaves ease toward you
from my heartbeat?
Does it signify safe rhythm
in your long liquid sleep?
There is no sound from you,
no applause, no protest.
Are you dreaming
beneath transparent eyelids
smooth as shells?

Complacent stranger gathering strength
on a dark shore, every part
of you strives to be whole.
Would you lament if your small world
was cut down suddenly
like a brittle, out of season
harvest?

Discovering new fear
toward my own flesh and blood
as you silently puncture
my familiar security,

I am scared
of your quiet invasion,
of your blossoming steadily
and rising
to recreate my world.

RAIN

Tara L. Masih

Last night I listened to the torrent of rain
just outside
and thought
how different it sounds.
There are signs you are coming soon,
signs that show you are eager
to open the door
to your new world.
So today I prepare as if for a final ritual,
for this is an ending
as well as a beginning.
I rest from those tasks we busy ourselves with
when we can't be still,
drink white grape juice
feeling you jump
at the coolness.
I linger in your room, a space full of half-imagined expectations.
I wonder who you will be,
who you will become.
Last night your father and I filmed our messages to you
so you will someday see
your parents were once young
and so eager for you.

Last night I listened to the rain and thought
Soon, soon you will hear that beautiful noise, too.

MY SON DANIEL IS BORN AND WONDERS

Susan Thomas

You slipped and slurped,
did somersaults in the dark;
and when your time came
you dived down fast.
Bone scraped against bone.
Frantic, you came through.

We smile at you
among the rows of startled babies.
They lie dazed and quivering
in their plastic isolettes.
You chew your wrapped-up fists:
Why am I here? What happens next?

MY BABY

Janell Moon

She screams and cries and cries.
She whimpers.
She whines.
She startles.
She wiggles
free of zippers, buttons, elastic.

She rubs her eyes, pinches her mouth,
puckers.
She sags in my arms, flops down.
She lets go a squeak, a burp, a yawn.
Her chest heaves.
She wet drools.
She makes a warm place on me,
skin to skin.
She nods off. She falls over the edge.
She's asleep.

She's tired.
It's her first week on the job.

NAPOLEON'S CIGAR

DC Berry

I'd been out gigging frogs and snakes
and gars and smoking cheap
stogies that doubled as mosquito spray;

and to get back into my room, at three
AM, I thought, "Why not return the way I left,
through my window?" So, I removed the screen.
Miss Kitty didn't screech
or hiss. Nor my desert-prophet mother,
standing there like a sheet,

but talking good sense, "Easier
to use the front door, son."
Now she tells me! I was doing scissors:

one leg out the window, one in.
Her logic like a hook surprised
me so, I flopped into the room.

My breath knocked out, I lay there and gurgled
like a decked fish, like a catfish. I had
about as many whiskers, though none long enough

to make me look wise as a turd
wrestler off the bottom. Mother
did not ask what was on my breath.

She became my sister,
grew in reverse
till she was my toddler.

And, now, I've got a child. He lies
there in the dark like a ten-pound guppy,
mouth open; the pacifier dangling

like a lure falling from his mouth.
But not tonight. He's still our emperor.
He likes it here. I adjust the plastic

nipple, center it like I'm the butler,
and he gives it several quick puffs
like a cigar he'd almost let go out.

MASCULINITY MEETS HIS DAUGHTER

Todd Palmer

My macho days are over now.
Hard to believe
That rough and tumble self is really dead.
So many times before,
Like a stubborn brush fire,
My wild-eyed side burned through
Those wet, maternal blankets
Thrown by women meaning well.

Good-bye to my hard-driving, deep-sleeping dog,
Who caroused with the boys
And only played with manly toys,
The tempestuous, two-fisted me,
Who ran himself ragged time and again,
And muscled his way to the top of the heap,
To the jagged-edge cliff of self-reflection
Where he'd wrestle himself
And win,
Then stand tall, proud, and alone, looking down,
Laughing at life's little obstacles,
Tough as a he-man can be.

Strange how, not with a bang
But a whimper in that gentle,
Terrible, first good night
As a father bolt upright in bed
At the sound of my daughter's cry,
The macho me wandered away.

I now sing a rusty lullaby
To will her back to sleep.
But when her fever soars,

My blood runs cold with fear.
At night her coughing
Takes my breath away
Until she takes her next.
When she can't tell me where it hurts,
I feel the ache bone deep.

But awakened somewhere inside me
A maternal voice whispers,
This too will pass, my son.

Still, as my heart stops cold
At a bump in the night;
I perceive the house settling
As a serious threat,
And I look down on my daughter,
So fragile in the dark of night,
And marvel at the weight of change she brings.

My macho days are over now,
But I am the man of the house.

JESSE TEACHES HIS MOTHER

Claudia Van Gerven

to walk

suddenly you are aware of
legs and how air

catches, is a place
you travel

through, all the little
bones return

to your feet, are happy, take risks
you remember you

are falling, this is danger, but
you ride

backbone, ankles, and you
are hollering, are laughing because

you are here, you were
there, but now

you are here

GIRLS

MaryLee McNeal

The young girls play in the park
making a house of dry grass.
Inside they place a straw queen
they name "Odd Audrey."
Their laughter cuts through
the blue day.

Buds of breasts begin
under the shirt of one,
but my daughter and the others
are flat still, with childhood.
They are content with their
house, their game
of rolling down the grassy hill.

Soon they will all lose this game,
their voices will be muted,
their bodies become objects
for the world,
their beauty lost to themselves,
the possibilities of their new games
distant and dangerous.

I want to lock them
in their house with Odd Audrey,
all of them still honoring
their honest odd selves.
I dread that blood road
They must travel.
I've already gone down.

SCREENING

Ginnie Goulet Gavrin

He begged and pleaded
for this rite of passage
until I caved in.

My son's first "R" rated movie,
the one where the hero
is a spy, the good guy
who kills all the right people,
even the girl he makes love to
because it turns out—
she was bad after all.

Cars blow up—gasoline-blue streaks
soaring out of orange-gold flames
higher than the screen's squared-off sky.
A man is shot and left to die,
his eyes glazing into the hard stare
of his death, while blood pours,
liquid and red onto the gray
concrete beneath his head.

And all this before the opening credits,
tiny names appearing on the screen
in front of the sky blaze
while fast cars make a getaway
and bullets sing in our ears.

Then come stunts and sex;
more sex and stunts.
Through both, the dialogue
runs smart and pithy.

All the way home the boys recite
scripted one-liners, word for word,
correcting each others' mistakes,
getting it right—
their hero was never
at a loss for words.

Not the way I am, gripping
the steering wheel, listening
as they imitate a firing grenade,
turning their voices into weapons
that go off in their throats.

THE MONTH OF JUNE: 13½

Sharon Olds

As my daughter approaches graduation and
puberty at the same time, at her
own calm deliberate serious rate,
she begins to kick up her heels, jazz out her
hands, thrust out her hip bones, chant
I'm great! I'm great! She feels 8th grade coming
open around her, a chrysalis cracking and
letting her out, it falls behind her and
joins the other husks on the ground,
7th grade, 6th grade, the
purple rind of 5th grade, the
hard jacket of 4th when she had so much pain,
3rd grade, 2nd, the dim cocoon of
1st grade back there somewhere on the path, and
kindergarten like a strip of thumb-suck blanket
taken from the actual blanket they wrapped her in at birth.
The whole school is coming off her shoulders like a
cloak unclasped, and she dances forth in her
jerky sexy child's joke dance of
self, self, her throat tight and a
hard new song coming out of it, while her
two dark eyes shine
above her body like a good mother and a
good father who look down and
love everything their baby does, the way she
lives their love.

THE FORMALITY

Peter E. Murphy

At the Eighth Grade Prom which I got suckered into chaperoning
the pubescent couples arrive in stretch limos that let them out
in the play ground near the swings and teeter board.
The girls in expensive gowns stutter on heels, click their gum,
their heads molded in permanent waves, dips, storms, beehives,
honey doo's, as their corsaged breasts swell and flower.
One strikes a Madonna pose, pushes herself up
as if it were the next day and the asphalt were a beach
blanket and she, the darling fun girl surrounded by bronze brutes,
each begging her to save the last wave for him.

Inside, the gym is a jungle of crepe paper which the boys climb
to strip the balloons from their branches and put them in their mouths,
sucking helium to make their transparent voices whistle like
    cartoon drunks.
They group and push around the cooler of coke, shaking the cans
    before popping
them open to spray themselves and their dates whose satin dresses stain
like wounds. One young lady chases them over the tables, screams
I'll kill you, you scum sucking douche bags! While the principal
    glad-hands
the parents who have come to tape their new men, new women.

If only my daughter were not part of this. Streaming from one ring
to another, whispering among the princesses, converging on the tribe
of barbarians—she gestures to the one who wears his cap backwards,
the one whose dirt brown shirt comes loose from his pants
as they begin to move to the hip hop, as they wrap themselves
in its icy tubes of war music. I see how he looks her over, jumping
up and down before her polished smile, how his eyes say, Me hungry,
Me need to eat. Other bodies follow them into the whirl beneath
the mock chandelier which twists the spotted light and fractures it
over their bodies, as they rock their heads, stretch their arms
toward the flashing sky, open their mouths as if to inhale, as if to shout,
as if to taste the honey of their June-new flesh.

WORKING PAPERS

Linda Simone

Your birth certificate
Was **my** working paper—
No pay, three shifts,
No vacation.

Menial jobs
No one else wanted—
Except sometimes dad—
For nearly 15 years.

Today, we're going
For **your** working papers—
Permit to hand off
A nine iron or a Big Mac.

No matter.
You'll learn something.
My man-in-training
So handsome, kind, talented.

Does this mean a pink slip
In my future
From the best damn job
I ever had?

Perhaps not yet,
But we're all
Replaceable—
Aren't we?

Here's my blessing:
May the fruits of your labor
Be as exquisite
As the fruits of mine.

RITES OF PASSAGE

Barbara Crooker

My daughter takes her driving test,
and I wait by the fence,
chained by all the old fears.
She drives off with the inspector,
Squinty eyed, critical.
Be kind, I pray, this is my little girl.
I glimpse them in the distance,
traversing the maze of stop signs, yields,
pylons. She pivots into the k-turns,
grips the wheel too tight.
From this distance, they could be on a ride
in an amusement park: The Flying Dutchman,
The Wild Mouse, The Runaway Train.
She's white lipped with fear and pleasure;
I'm down here on earth, stomach in a fist,
fear tap dancing staccato on my heart.
They never told me in the hospital
that this cord could not be cut.
The silver car returns, bringing them back.
He tips his hat, hands her the forms.
She passes! She's a driver!
And off we go, careening through
the rest of our tangled lives.

THE KNOWING

Sue Ellen Thompson

The night before the final exam,
I stand in her doorway, my arms filled
with laundry still taut from the line.
High school is almost over, everything
littering her room is broken or ending:
the cupped stubs of candles,
the wilted root-hairs of a cactus
spilled on the sill in a scattering of sand;
the confetti that's left when notes are torn
from their bindings speckling the carpet
like so many used-up stars.
She sits in a cross-legged slump on the floor,
her baseball cap pulled down low
and her Baudelaire propped open
with a shoe. If she needs
my help, she's not asking. When she

was in seventh grade, I bought her
Les Chateaux de France at a bookstall in Paris.
Night after night we sat propped in her bed,
one of us reading until she came
to an unfamiliar word and the other
looking it up in the old blue Larousse. By the end
of that winter we knew the word for *corbel*
and *truss, portcullis* and *finial*
and *crenelation.* Between us we had
all the knowledge we needed to live in a world
whose walls contained everything
worth desiring. I lay the clothes

in a fragrant heap at her feet. Without looking up,
she aims the remote at her stereo, clicks,
and a chorus of angry voices erupts
all around us. When I was her age,

I would study hard up until bedtime,
then close the book, knowing
there was a point beyond which the facts
could not take me. So later that evening,
when her light goes out and I turn out mine,
together we enter that time when all
we can know of each other is already
inside us, and who can conceive
a word for what lies ahead?

I FORGOT MY GLOVES

Krista Hauenstein

When I'm eating dinner with my parents
in their house, the one I grew up in,
I want to tell them *I love you,*
or *Thank you.* Mostly, I ask for more
carrots, perhaps another potato, never
more milk. My dad asks about work;
I complain. My mom asks about boys;
I lie. I want to tell them *I miss wiener roasts
in the living room, Walt Disney on TV.*
My brother asks for beer;
my sister wants to shop for rings.
I don't want her to think of boys.
They all excuse themselves for phone calls,
homework, showers; I'm left alone
still chewing my steak, with my parents
watching. I want to say *I'll move back home;
please pay my bills.* I tell them
about my roommate's new faith—a cult,
led by her boyfriend's mother, where even
marriage is no longer worth the effort,
certainly sex is not. They shake their heads,
want to ask why I don't go to church.
They used to take me every Sunday,
dress me in pink and patent-leather,
tie my hair up in braids, shuffle me in the car
with my brothers in little boy suits.
When my mom offers me a brownie
with powdered sugar for dessert, I pass,
say I am stuffed, ask to take some home,
wanting to say, *This will always be home.*
I leave, making sure to kiss each cheek,
knowing I'll call before I fall asleep
to substitute *I forgot my gloves on the front table*
for *I love you* and *Thank you.*

WEDDING DAY

Jacqueline Kudler

I

The day plays down to waiting:
my dress, ready, drapes the closet door—
the mothers are wearing burgundy tonight—
my suede shoes, burgundy, below,
toe in to the rim of the rug,
my hair—already coaxed, coiled
high on my head, is caught
with a burgundy bow.

All afternoon, snow
piles down the December sky,
gathers to a white wool on the window
ledge, as all the days gather
to this all but last one of the year,
your wedding day,

as all I know
of the word, act,
"mother" gathers
to this doing
of not doing,
move of countermove,
this way of waiting.

II

A sudden flutter at the door
and you standing there—
your face painfully open,
with your new haircut
and your thumbnail
to be fixed,

95

that old action
between us, easy—
easy at the first:
sleek skin insulted at
knee, finger, elbow,
Tonka truck, wounded
at the wheel,

that old action between us:
the mercurochrome,
the cookie, the kiss,
the fix no longer mine
to give.

How good it is—
your long thumb
steady in my left hand,
scissors lifted in my right—
to pare away the offending
crescent, even out
the edge.

III

If at the first
there was nothing to you
but wanting, small wonder
the habit of wanting for you
followed so soon after—
I settled as easy into it
as that old tartan lap robe,
the one big enough to cover
us both.

It is no small
comfort to me, then,
that the girl you got
is the girl you wanted,
the one you waited for,
the way your tux, tails,

patent wing tips wait in my
closet, patient, preening
for the first dance,

and as if today
you were finished with
waiting, finished with wanting,
I feel a stillness in your fingers,
the answering stillness
In mine.

STEPFATHER

Michael Cleary

I swear, your mother doesn't snore, she purrs.

So time has another trick up its sleeve.
Widow weds widower. Catholic and Jew.
Happily ever after   after
unhappy endings they've been through.

Once more we've come home to roost
at the kitchen table, four chairs left
holding up under thirty years of family.
Our baker's half dozen.   A game of
musical chairs that never stops;
we slouch against doorjambs;
perch on countertops.   All our lives
we have crowded this room with our need.
Hunger and thirst, confessions and lies,
glorious insults, uproarious laughs,
comings and goings and going nowheres.
Our mother clucking over her wayward brood,
making the best of things.   Making do.

Stepfather, stranger, thief—
we've come home to make do with you.
As if our blessing forgave you for living
in the shadow of a father's ghost.

Good man.   Gentle man.
Try to understand: we are uneasy
with your joy,   newly-wed
secrets unlocked like treasure
left behind in the marriage bed.
Jesus, Mary, and Joseph—
how many times must we learn
how much we can never know?

Tonight, unsleeping, you will turn
from our mother's purring sleep
wondering
if it was always so
or it is you who brings her such content.
And we, in strangely familiar beds,
will listen into that other darkness
remembering
all the things our father never said.

SO NOW

Carol Wade Lundberg

there is to be
another body
flowing from the body
that once curled
like a shell
in my inland sea.

How strange
this unfolding outward
like the whorls
of planets
into bright rings
of life.

When a wave
separates herself
from the body
of her mother
crests and disappears
into another
constellation

does the sea mourn
as she rejoices?
Imperceptibly
her child has been flowing
toward an inevitable
transformation.

Each birth reminds
us that the tides
have shifted.
It is not
a daughter's
birth that separates

her from her mother
but the moment
she releases her
own child
to the world.

CHILDHOOD

Elizabeth Spires

Once, without form or substance, I answered the call,
stepping into the light, into my body.
Only there could I eat and sleep and dream.
Only there could I touch and be touched back,
mouthing the world's words, my voice
                              unspooling inside me.

The season of childhood is summer,
summer's long days, the children at play
on the long lawns wearing their bodies
like shields that dare to reflect the sun.
It was our country for a little while,
we were each, in our time, its first citizen,
and now I turn to look back into it
as one might gaze from a cloud-ridden parapet
                              into a distant kingdom.

I stand among the mothers as they call
their children to *Come in, come in right now.*
How is it that I am here?
When did I change from this to that?
Who changed me? A child, a daughter,
                              answering the call.

There, in the falling dusk, beyond my reach,
she slips in and out of shadow, seeking
the others out, joining a circle of unbroken hands
that lightly dance around the twilit emptiness.
But from each lighted house a mother calls a name,
a child drops out, and night descends, how quickly
                              night descends.

And I hear my voice rise up against the mothers
and what the mothers stand for:
Let the children's game never end.
Let them fall, exhausted, where they stand,
the dew staining their clothes,
the moon on their bodies like a hand.
Let them dream marvelous dreams
as they sleep, immortal, in the long grass.
Let everything remain as it is!

MOTHERS AND DAUGHTERS

Maude Meehan

There is a cord between us
not yet cut
On it we move
like tightrope walkers
novices
uncertain of the net
Take tentative steps
across the gulf
toward one another
Careful
not wishing to turn back
Hopeful
that keeping balance
we can meet
can then embrace
and pass each other
as we must

CHANGE OF SEASONS

Miriam Pederson

"Perk up," your mother would say,
her hand lifting your chin
as if this gesture
could elevate your mood
or stop revelations about the world.
And for a moment her magic worked,
for she knew your heart better than anyone.
To know and be known, that is what you lose
as the middle of life
edges toward the margins,
as your husband falls ill,
as sleep, shallow and tentative,
threatens to abandon your nights,
as familiar trees become strange,
refusing to turn or allow their leaves to fall
even in the depth of November.
And now, your mother has nearly forgotten your name.
Her face still cheerful and full of light,
she thanks you for coming,
takes your hand, and says goodbye.

CHRISTMAS IN TUSCON

Jeff Worley

We don't mean to do it,
my brothers and I,
but we grow bald

in front of our father.
Our bellies billow like sails,
forcing him to drift further

and further away from us.
The wrinkles around our eyes:
inscrutable hieroglyphs.

Everybody gets older
and perhaps, we like to think,
happier with less.

We'd be happy to see him
effortlessly raise his glass
of Rattlesnake Beer and toast

the moonlit saguaro
as it sharpens into the next
century. Then we'd wish,

long months or years later,
for him to simply drift away
during one of Harry's off-

key 7th inning stretches. Now,
Dad shifts uncomfortably
in the back-porch Bacalounger,

Searches for something,
The channel changer perhaps.
His legs are brittle as driftwood.

I feel him floating back and back.
"Do you remember that time

in Abilene...?" I begin. "Of course,"
he says, still searching. "Of course I do."

MY IMMIGRANT MOTHER TRANSPLANTED

Judy Kronenfeld

She always seemed at home
in the city. Pushcarts bloomed
in the alleys, black flakes
spiraled down from chimneys
eloquently as snow. She waded
fearlessly into the litter
of subway toilets, she shooed it away
like a mongrel; out of her purse
came ready Kleenex
and consecration of the seat.
She watched the seasons
on a single fenced tree.

Now we take her to the Sierras,
offer her nature close up.
On the way, she praises mountains,
Tyrolean forests,
where flowers grow at regular intervals
and the grass is as clean
as the sidewalks of Salt Lake.
She sniffs the idea of air
in the air-conditioned car.
When we stop she takes a polite breath,
Ah, mountain air—refreshing.
And when we suggest the quarter-mile stroll,
easy, pine-forested, cool,
she walks quickly,
as she used to in dark alleys,
pulling her shawl around her,
in the yellow dust of pines.

LIVE LONG, DIE SHORT

J. B. Bernstein

I watch my mother each day
in her hospital bed hovering
in a twilight zone, sinking slowly
into the dead of night. During that week
she smiles once, and I think:
She's getting better. But I know
her smile is one of resignation,
not resurrection.

By the sixth day
her breathing strains as if she's
in hard labor waiting, praying
to deliver, to be delivered.

And on the seventh day,
I change her status from Code C
to D (this is not the alphabet I learned
in Kindergarten) so that drugs
can set her free. Soon, her knotted limbs
unfold easily onto the cool white sheets,
the same way a tired baby accepts
the comfort of a crib.

And I stand by watching.
And her eyes, her eyes open unblinking
for an eternity, as wide as I have ever
seen before, ready to devour the world.
Then they close.

RESPONSIBILITIES AND EXPECTATIONS

GIVER OF FORMS

Robin L. Smith-Johnson

The still part of the day
is the hardest. It is my hour of wanting
to flower, to burst out singing
or to undress wildly in front of the window.
Nothing moves but my blood and the minute hand.

In childhood, I dreamed of growing up
and bearing children. Now with two
of my own, I cradle my young body
if only in dreams. Indian goddess,
I have infinite arms, all moving, giving.

It is a life of no mercy.
My mouth sprouts beanstalks
and giants. Just one more, they plead.
The words become my mantra:
Once upon, on, om.

I give myself over as whole:
then fragment when
the baby cries, the phone rings,
the sirens shriek:
it's over, it's over.

I fold myself away
like a shirt that
won't be worn again
until summer.

THE INVENTION OF CHILDHOOD

Stefan Kiesbye

On Tuesdays,
Dad drove me down to soccer practice.
"I'll be back soon," he assured Mom
who was laying the table for supper;
she believed in three meals a day.
"Boy, you're going to love this,"
he assured me.
In town, he stopped
in front of the big department store
where a mechanical bear blew bubbles.
At the snack bar we ate hot dogs and fries,
"like cowboys after a long day
on the cattle trail," he said.
Dad knew I wouldn't tell Mom.
I was grateful for his confidence,
my mouth full of hot fries
I couldn't swallow or chew.
In front of the locker room, he made
me throw the ball at him and headed it back.
He told me, "Knock 'em dead,"
and went home to Mom and supper
and television. I missed *Family Affair,*
missed orphaned Jody, Buffy, Cissy
and bear-like Uncle Bill.
I hoped Dad wouldn't find out
I had been a failure in soccer
and didn't practice any more.
In the backyard of our house,
he had proudly taken pictures of me
with a new ball and in full uniform,
blue shirt, white pants, blue socks.
These were the first photos in color—
they have faded to red and yellow;
our lives, it seems, were taking place
in one permanent sunset.

QUESTIONS FOR
MY GROWN CHILDREN

Maude Meehan

Is it a burden that I ache along with you,
share not just your joy, but pain?
And do you know how much I want to be
all that you wish, and yet how much
I sometimes balk at expectations,
real or unfounded, and imagine
that the same holds true for you?

Does it make you uneasy to be so loved,
and does it sometimes comfort you?
It is the only love without condition
I have ever known or given.
And in your middle age, my old,
can you be patient with me, and accept it,
and can we keep the closeness we have shared?

X

Doyle Wesley Walls

My son only wants to type the "x" on the screen.
He holds his finger down:
xxxxxxxxxxxxxxxxxxxxxxxxxxxxxxxxxxxxxxxxxxxxx.
I'm tired, overworked, and now angry with him.
"No," I say. "Either write something
or stop wasting my time."

He's disappointed. In time, he types,
"I ws luking at the stars last niht."

I leave, return. He's gone back to
xxxxxxxxxxxxxxxxxxxxxxxxxxxxxxxxxxxxxxxxxxxxx.
Perhaps it's something
that has to be said, something
he can never finish writing,
each "x" one time
when our paths crossed.

What thunder I roared tonight,
what a scene when he ate
without closing his mouth,
without eating over his plate!
He waves the tines of his fork
near his eyes and
interrupts when my wife or I talk!
Yesterday on his trike
he almost ran over
the two-year-old Sarah!

He's five. How many times
must I repeat myself?
Be kind! Be careful! Think!
In 5th grade Jon suggested
we slam the door on Annette,

who was to hold the door for us all,
as we walked past her into class.
The two boys in front of me did, and
the third time is automatic.
I didn't think she'd be hurt.
I didn't think.
Mrs. Muldrew, livid, singled me out,
made me look up at her, said
she expected more from me than that.

Seth's asleep. I'm walking
under stars. I stop and force myself
to look up.
I always thought I'd be
a stellar daddy.
Go on, stupid, I think to myself,
*you know who you are, write your name,
write your name, stupid.*

With the heel of my shoe
I make my "x" in the sandbox. I fill
the box with "x" after "x" for the many
times I have been cross with him here
on the playground.

It is so far from this sandbox to
the stars. The way they shine.

WHEN STILLNESS DROPS

Susan Clayton-Goldner

Because time ridicules and praise isn't enough,
I think of my daughter's college friend,
a single mother. "It's so hard," she says.
And I envision her race from philosophy to daycare,
shift of gears as through streaked windows
she identifies passing objects for her son.
Tearing bite-sized pieces of chicken from the bone
for dinner, brush of lips across scraped knee.

No other person to lift her chin with a fingertip,
whisper, "good job,' or "I'll take over now."
And all the while the sun climbs and drops
endlessly behind a thin haze of persistent stars.
Tolerant and caring for the hundredth time,
she tests the bath water with an elbow.
Her textbook wedged between porcelain,
strips him quickly, like opening a window.
His small limbs bronzed and twirling.

Later, greedy for slumber, she will lie down
next to him and drift away, dream herself altered
beyond recognition, buried somewhere
under the moist sleep of childhood.
And in that great collapsible moment when motion stops,
she remains as vulnerable as he, though knowing
the names of a hundred thousand objects,
an inventory of states of mind she cannot label.

While I, accustomed to the barren space
where womb once lay, can't pity my emptiness.
Knowing, as the Navajos do, I am a bridge
for my young sisters. Pregnant with the rain children,
they link hands and sweep across the sky,

an invisible labor that bathes the world.
Attached to the placenta moon by a thin cord of light,
I know there are mothers for every living thing.
And the ocean is a mother, too, soothing us with ballads
long after we have ceased to listen. I pause and bend
toward the navy blue breast of sky, tilt my head to the wind,
the steady beat of the world's mending heart.

SCOURED

David Starkey

My two daughters chase each other
in the Laundromat, past the banks
of Speedqueens, between
the industrial Wash-o-matics.
They dart after loose buttons
and puffs of lint, gifts
they bring to me.

Christ!
A hundred dollars for a used machine,
and I can't come up with it.
God's benediction upon these children,
but I wish they would vanish,
I want the power to leave
at a moment's notice, the power
to tear down every single wall in my house.

I want to be as clean as fresh laundry.
I want a shell
that's hard and whorled so deep
I cannot hear the beat
and drum of poverty
thumping
like a clump of wet clothes in a dryer:
I want, I want.

I have nothing at all to give.

DADS WITH KIDS

Brian Daldorph

Sunday mornings it's our turn,
after getting away from them all week.
New men all,
surrogate mothers,
we take our kids to the park,
pretending
we'd rather not be home
watching the big game.
While kids run crazy
as footballers without
rules pads helmets
trying to hurt themselves,
we exchange words—
not the easy chat
we have with skilled young mothers.
But there are the college frisbee girls
twirling in the sun,
watching us, we think,
being good dads,
college girls who, perhaps,
go for older men,
men they dream are good with kids
every day of the week.

SO THERE *(excerpt)*

Naomi Shihab Nye

the three-year-old wore twenty dresses
to her preschool interview

her mother could not make her
change

take some off her mother pleaded
and the girl put on a second pair of tights

please I'm begging you
what will they think of us

the girl put all eight of her pastel barrettes
into her hair at once

she put on
her fuzzy green gloves

she would have worn four shoes but could not
get the second pair on top of the first pair

her mother cried you look like a mountain
who has come to live with me

she had trouble walking
from the car up to the school

trouble sitting
in the small chair that was offered

the headmistress said
my my we are a stubborn personality

FIRST CHORE

J.B. Safford

Riding on a tongue of sunlight
she can't see
the little girl crouches
and makes her own balled shadow.
She sobs inside the barn door
opened wide on winter,
an eight year old crying in stereo
across the barn yard to where
the cats wail too. Lambs bleat
in some sympathetic chorus
in the far corner of the shed.
Three horses look up from their feeding.
She crouches on knees
now darkened by tears
shoveling down
into two heaving shoulders.
All in response to a chore assigned.
To sweep up the loose straw
into one meticulous
mound. Nothing has been done
about it. The broom leans against
the closed stall door
and she continues to cry,
to cry even harder, against
the way the world wants her.

HOUSE RULES

Joanna C. Scott

It's amazing what a few words on a page can do
this son my husband brought me back from Inch'on
is sixteen-and-a-half now and getting seriously itchy
which is as it should be however being his mother
and responsible because his father is in Bangkok
en route to Hong Kong Shanghai Ho Chi Minh City
when he came in blossoming with cigarette smoke at ten-forty
and school out at two-fifteen no phone call nothing
just a message with his sister which is not allowed
I won't be late then was unconscionably late
that's when son and mother had a little come-to-Jesus meeting
mother laying down the law and son all spit and argument
it didn't work so down I sits and types up the House Rules
lays them on him they looked official and were received that way
he walked about with them in his hand reading them like a scholar
who has just been handed the lost Dead Sea scrolls a kind of
taken-aback respectfulness then went off with them into his room
and shut the door it must have been an hour later when he showed up
by my bed face anxious stuttering that he would like to switch
Wednesday with Thursday because his friend works Thursday
after school that was three weeks ago and he's been home
every night on schedule and proud it's just amazing
how a few words on a page can seem inscribed in stone
no wonder Moses' face shone when he came down
from the mountain with the ten commandments in his hand.

SPIDERS KEEP HOUSE

Susan Steger Welsh

"Sleep is the gift of spiders."—Carl Sandburg

I envy those spiders,
how they set their tables and wait,
disguise themselves as centerpieces.
Tonight, as I wait in a cabin for sleep,
I cannot find the center of anything.

The night is blind, as spiders are.
I pick my way carefully
through sounds that bang at the screen:
A breeze, sweet breath of forest.
Creatures scrambling leaves.
Shrieks and shufflings—a lull.
My mother, crouching in the pine cones,
Speaking Polish, trying to explain to God
why I never dream about her.
Not once in 19 years. Overhearing this,

I feel again her hands toweling me dry
after a bath. She brushes my hair straight,
tells me what a good father I have, that I must
be good, too, since God was holding her
accountable for my still-damp soul.

I spend years slipping out of the clothes she dressed me in.

In families and in cabins, cobwebs
hold up the corners. Their gauzy ruins
float like chiffon scarves, the ghostly wave
of the mothers who made them, spiders
who breathed softly through their stomachs
and made plans at night, working patiently

to repair the damage of the day, their webs
knit of holes, strong silk
knotted around the empty places.

The spiderlings wake up to find
their mothers gone. They let the wind pull
the silk out, follow the tug
into the drop and sway,

into the center of their lives.

LIVING ROOM

Floyd Skloot

I thought the face of Beethoven glaring
between our piano and easy chair
was my father when he was young. Staring
till his eyes dried up, sparking the wild hair
that would soon fly completely off his head,
my father even then was a wizard
of silent menace, a genius of dread.
He saw me. He knew what I did. He heard
the music of my musings. My mother
played Gershwin oblivious of the scorn
singing along would bring down on me. Her
smile froze, her eyes slowly closed, her voice worn
down by years of smoke broke into sobs when
she lost herself in the old melody.
Not me. I sat beside her silently.

POLISHING STONES

June Owens

You were once a little pebble rocked in
The waters of my womb. And so I tried to be your
Ocean, smooth the stones of youth's bewilderment,
Refine them into manageable grains. I showed you
Owl wings pressed on snow where the rabbit
Had paused a breath too long, and I said be careful
And you asked of what. I took you to train
Tunnels where in August mosses and frogs clung
To cold dark wet granite, and only thin tracks
Gave off light and I spoke to you of safety
In the straight and narrow and you said for whom.
We sang songs all of my choosing. There were
Music and art and opera, poems and stacks
Of books, all my notions of what was worthy.
But you withdrew perplexed and yowling why.
For years you tumbled in my lapidary. I did not
Know it smoothed away the unsmooth shapes that
Made yourself your self. I wanted you polished
Perfect as an agate marble, did not see your
Swirling dreams get locked inside a piece
Of round rock.

None of it worked: you look at me now and your
Pupils empty and fill, go dark as tunnels,
Hop into nightmares and jagged landmarks and ripping tides
And avalanches of dead dreams and no songs.
Still, we have not, oh, we have not failed!
The irises of your eyes drugged big as black
Moons and the unsweet smell of your breathing
Are no defeat. Only innocence is lost.
There are ways back. The rising road
Has lain itself down for you. Let us, round
As love, roll upward, David, upward…

THE SON

Constance Pultz

Consider him
the way he is,
not as you'd planned him,
putting him together
in your mind
like a map of the world,
but as he might be
if he were someone else's son.

Pay attention to him,
to the way he looks at you
as if you were a stranger.
Tell yourself you are meeting
for the first time. Take his hand
(he may be willing)
and smile as if you were smiling
at someone you could learn
to love.

Mention your name
(he will remember).
He is not as alien
as you might think,
as long as you bear in mind
the fact that you made him
what he is, while trying
to make him into
something else.

MAKING IT IN AMERICA

Penny Cagan

1.

My father was the son of a trained Rabbi
turned grocer who withdrew to a dark prayer room
during all of his days in America, the son of
a full-cheeked Russian woman who bought real estate
in miserable neighborhoods and supported her family
with the rent. My father was the first to speak English
from the start, and he earned his money during summers
in the Catskills, when all the men were away at war,
and he learned something about life.
When he was in college his body pushed high
into his shoulders, and he tackled the extended
football field with a brown ball tucked
under his arm like a rough baby.
He struck at anyone who called him a dirty Jew,
and although he was the quarterback
he was kept from joining his team's fraternity.
Making it in America
meant making it into the flush black book
that sat as a weight on his nightstand for years
called *Famous Jewish Athletes*.

2

My father decided that it was a sin
for anyone who grew as tall as my brother
not to play basketball. He poured cement
for a court over our driveway and put up a hoop.
He pushed my brother out the door after supper,
strung strobes from the porch in overlapping
loops of light, and backed the cars to the edge
of the road to give my brother room to work

his dribble. *All it takes is practice*
he said each night as he checked my brother's
grip on the ball, *Nothing comes easy in this life.*

My brother never aimed for the laced hoop
that flapped around in the sky,
and caught the light of fireflies
when they landed on the pits of its rope.
He threw the orange ball against the plywood
slats of the garage door, and rattled the house
with his *slam slam slam.*

3.

In deep winter my father drove me to the pond
at the edge of Jacob's Creek Road.
He revved up the cold night air with his engine.
I spent a long time in the back seat
crossing the laces of my skates,
working up the curve of my foot,
pulling one end tight against my socks
and then the other,
until my feet felt as thick as the earth.
My father would propel me on the pond
with a strong lift of his arm,
and I would shake from the first slice of blades.
The way the metal cut the ice felt as dark
as the locked-up houses beyond the road
that vibrated from every window, and the trees
that turned down their necks in the woods.
Each time I fell and the ice stung through my bottom
My father would pull me up by the V of my elbow.
When you fall down you get up
he would say so often it felt like a prayer.
And he would push me off again and again
before the pink dust of the headlights
that unfolded like roses upon the frozen ice.

TENDERNESS

IN DAY CARE

Victor M. Depta

Another month of snow—
surprised, again, the south closed its schools
and my girl was in day care, crowded
expensive among the children as I dropped her off
waiting till she got to the door
before I crunched away in my chains.

Early one day, in a blizzard
I went to gather her up
in the warm-humid, milk-ginger room
and found the children on pallets, refugees of cookies
and my daughter crooning to them
lullabies, *Hush, little baby, don't you cry.*

The director shushed me
and then in the kitchen, babbled about my girl
what a grown-up little helper she really was.
The woman made me nervous.
Authority usually does

and I wished
cowering from her strong-armed, coy prattle
that I was in the day room
on the pallet with cookie breath
drowsy, drifting to sleep
in my child's care.

FIRST LOVE LETTER

gary blankenburg

It's a gray Saturday morning
& my son & I are walking in the rain
toward the canopy above the entrance
to Hunt Valley Mall.
He splashes on ahead of me to the big blue
mailbox off to the side—all slick & wet,
& I watch him slide his letter in, let go
of the handle, open it again to see the envelope
disappeared, let it swing closed again, & turn to me.

He's waited twenty-four hours to post this carefully
hand-printed letter. He addressed, stamped, & sealed
it w/out allowing me to read it. It's a love letter
he says to an older girl in the fourth grade who rides
his bus & sometimes smiles at him.

He has mailed his letter in spite of the advice
from his friend Tommy who told him that she would break
his heart just like she broke Sean's heart,
& he asks me if I think that will happen.
I don't ever lie to him, so I say, *Probably,*
Sooner or later, but it will be worth it.
And he seemed content with that answer,
So we headed inside to play at Space Port Video Arcade
& then to Kay Bee Toys to buy a Robo Cop figure & vehicle
that he's wanted because it can fire a cap a second & is silver.

Later in the car on the way home I tease him
& ask if he wants to go back to the mall & buy a Barbie Doll.
He laughs & punches me in the arm,
& then after a mile or two of silence says, *You know,*
Daddy, when I was a little boy I did have a Barbie Doll
that I used to take into the bathtub w/me,

136

but mostly I just liked taking off her clothes
& looking at her pillows.

And I am suddenly struck with a hunger & a realization
that of all her other obvious anatomical assets & limitations
Barbie has no nipples on her breasts & could never give
suckle or comfort to any child or man, & I find myself missing
both at once my mother & his.

ESSENTIAL LOVE

Rob Hardy

Place the palm of your hand
flat against your cheek,
push outward against
the inside
with your tongue—
this is how it feels, only
smoother, tighter,
rounder. And you know
your tongue's a tongue—
but what's this?
An elbow? A knee?
In another darkness you began
with familiar contours,
a specific fondness
for the sweet curve
of a jaw, the soft
inside of a thigh.
From these known shapes
your touch adjusts
to a shared darkness,
feeling out the intricate love
you have shaped
between yourselves.
But to these kicks
you extend a general love,
a love which requires
no other definition.
Birth will complicate
this love, too, with details—
but for now it simply
is.

PERCEPTIONS

Marlaina B. Tanny

Daughter, you were born during the generation
of those who debated whether a soul is present
in the womb; whether life is life.
Your soul visited me years before the actual
conception, and like so many times
in the years now, you did not call out
but, separate and free nearby, waited
to be claimed. I heard you
even though it was only your back that I saw
in the dream, knowing as I do, the words of silence
when one cannot find the syllables
or bear the rawness of our own incomplete voice.

As you took shape for this beguiling world,
I could feel the hesitation of your pre-thoughts.
Questions grew alongside your blossoming limbs.
There seemed a yearning from you as if
already you were a child alone in a large house
looking out into an even larger world.
I imagined your face pressing against the veined
wall of the sack and straight into my soul.
But I should have known the magnitude of your fear,
a demon that I also share.
I was frightened.
There were no lids to close your eyes.

Your depth cascaded like many drops through piled
stones into a somber pool.
For nine months we were the same water.
When you were born your arrival was announced not
by tears but by the desperate sound

as you sucked your wrinkled fist.
With equal will you secured to my breast.
Go back to that depth now daughter,
It is your strength. You will not become lost.
The darkness is the light.

BABY BY DAY

Wyatt Townley

1.

You wake to your own cry
and lie among the dinosaurs
on the sheets of your crib.

The world pours in, the dance
of the mobile above you,
walls strewn with alphabets,

family portraits tilting
above your dresser and the noise
of Dadda! trotting

in to make baby talk
to you, who have sailed
ancient seas all night.

2.

All day is a river of toys
rolling from your hands

to every bend in the house.
Behind the bookshelves, under

the sofa some vanish forever,
and still you keep laughing,

bobbing up against me
like a boat in its berth.

3.

As night falls you are safe
inside the tugboats
of the favored pajamas.

The lights go out ten
at a time across the city
and we each lie down to drift

to the land where thieves
and children and old men and tigers

get married. Above the tiny world,
God bless us, Orion rides.

A POEM FOR JESSE

David Zeiger

Raising you to my shoulder
for the obligatory burp
after four ounces of formula,
your head bobbing till I cradle it
in my palm, I begin to know again
this long-forgotten pleasure.
Worn out with lifting, carrying,
putting down a bundle of satin flesh,
I am an old man baffled by my appetite
for bonding with an eleven-week old.

Pained by the fretting,
charmed by my baptism with urine,
saddened by the harsh necessity
of our future parting,
I can't remember ever feeling so sure
about what's comic, what's tragic.

"It's hard to be a baby,"
I tell you—as you make demands
ill-understood while lying flat
on your back submitting to wet kisses.
When your stomach stutters,
or hiccups shake your tiny frame,
we mistake your grimace for a smile.
You pump your arms and legs in the air
as if to assert your will,
but I fear life will teach you
how the world turns a deaf ear.

You do not love me yet, and we
have not yet spoken,
but you lock my finger in your fist

as if you care,
not minding I am over the hill
and ready to give me a second chance.
As I stand and watch you sleep,
I am loud with dreams.

FOR ALISSA

Peter Cooley

This is a poem for my daughter,
her of the topaz eye reflecting mine
eight years into the world.
Women have told me my eyes are like a statue's,
unmoving, cold. Hers never stop dancing.

Nor does her little body
lost to a plie or the dark woods
in the midst of Brothers Grimm
surrender its sharp grip
on the ground under it, spinning.
Nor on the wind over her always lifting.

Who from her mother was ripped
before her time and clung to Death
three days until he fell.
Who cocks her head like a bear cub
at my approach, moving too fast
that I should touch her with my expectation.

Who in a night season
seven years back
when I lay in terror of myself
cried out and drew me to her
hours while I walked her.
That tiny head pressed to my shoulder
downed with hair fine as cowslip
or the soft, white fire of milkweed
spilling over my skin—
and lifted these wings here
nubby, oracular, stubborn,
which brought me to morning,
nudging their small way upward.

HOW TO CUT YOUR CHILD'S HAIR AT HOME

Rebekah Wolman

1.

With calm voice and patient hands
since sitting still will make her itch and squirm
toward the flinching point of the long shears
and it will take forever

2.

Artfully
so that your mother-in-law
the grandmother for whom the child is named
won't judge
might even quietly approve

3.

Outdoors in warm weather
telling her that mother birds
will use the hair to build their nests
each fair curl a promise
floating across the summer afternoon

4.

With what you know as love
and she might someday
write this poem

ORION'S BELT

Ann E. Michael

It is dark enough. Just.
He's too young to watch the late night sky,
but we walk out together
past dusk, onto the cool grass,
leaves beneath our feet.
He's wearing his pajamas
under his coat. He thinks he sees
Orion's belt, there; no, there.
It's funny how, at first,
All stars look alike.

Our necks begin to ache,
so I lie down. Earth is cold.
I make a blanket of myself
to keep him from the chill.
His hair tickles my chin.
We find the Little Dipper first,
then the big one. The Drinking Gourd.
The Bear.

It doesn't look like a bear, he says.
But there, those three bright stars
do make a shining belt in heaven.
His feet are cold, my muscles stiff—
we make an awkward constellation on the lawn.
He says he sees Orion's dagger
hanging from the belt; perhaps he does,
his eyes are better than mine.
Still, there's haze tonight
and too much glimmer from the city
and the rising moon.

I think about Orion, who cannot feel
the grass and cool leaves brush his skin or
a child's weight upon his body.
I hold my son against myself,
against the cold, against the earth,
against the darkness.
And from this night on, the stars are different:
named, found, loved,
recognizable in their sky.

PRE-ADOLESCENCE

Ann E. Michael

Your big cousin takes you aside
to tell of sly, handsome men
who follow blondes and
love dark women with green eyes.
She talks of spending their passion
while you wonder what she means,
listening to her stories
and putting on lipstick, in secret.
It strikes you that
you will need to be beautiful
to enter such a world,
remote, darkly dangerous,
overly perfumed.
You take Mother aside to tell
about new makeup shades, of how
"wineglow" is considered very becoming
on darker blondes but she says
you're still too young for that.
She asks what you've been reading;
her face is plain and
her face is beautiful, and
you cannot tell her anything.

AT TWELVE

Elizabeth McLagan

Late night, you and the dog
nose into my bed, flinging
your arm across me,
careful of my pillows
of breasts, you are too old
to be here,
but I let you stay.

Your hand settles
the neutral range
of my chest, I soothe your hair
like flame, the pale field
above your eyes.

Already, the man-smell
of cumin and sage
burns off your skin
like forkfuls
of earth turned
at the first of spring.

Sideways, under the covers,
we are parallel ridges,
a fixed topography,
the dog's dark body
working a basin
between us.

Soon you will leave
the bed of your childhood,
the way you left
my body, back
where we began,

and the dog will shift
from the lair of dreams
and travel between us, messages
spilled from her musky breath,
from the delicate pink
of her tongue.

MY SON'S FOOT

Gayle Brandeis

Today, I read a story
by Margaret Atwood
about how to like men.
It ends with the narrator
looking at her husband's foot
as it sticks out from under a sheet,
and loving him for that naked
foot, for the very fact that foot
was born. I felt such a shock
of recognition reading this,
because the same thing happened to me
last night with my son Arin.
Arin's foot was sticking out over the edge
of the bunk bed, and it almost broke
my heart to see that naked, vulnerable sole,
its living tissue, circling blood,
that foot that was once curled
in my belly, folded back against
his wet fetus shins—the sight of it
made me love him with an intensity
I have not felt since he was a baby.
That sweet foot, as bald and alone
as anything I've ever seen in this world,
his foot, not mine, not anything
I can claim, the foot that will walk
my son away from me and into his own
life.

WHY SOME NIGHTS I GO TO BED WITHOUT UNDRESSING

Elisavietta Ritchie

(For poets Josephine Jacobson, Rod Jellema, Irene Rouse, Roland Flint, Barri Armitage, and David and Judy Ray, who lost sons and a grandson in automobile accidents)

Even as my children scale
jungle-gym and pine,
they too are swinging toward silence.

In desperate dreams I try to save
my daughter from the flood of night.
Still she drowns and drowns

while both my sons
spin nightmare wheels
against a thundering sky.

This wet midnight terribly awake
I pace the living room. My youngest son
is driving his broken Toyota home

from the Grateful Dead Live In Concert.
The storm keeps pouring over icing streets.
Finally I go to bed

but toss, alert for doors or else
strange strained voices on the phone,
and I do not undress.

ONE TRUE LIFE

Barbara Hendryson

Walking to the neighborhood store,
my small, beautiful dog
straining at his red leash, and I
in my big winter jacket
against an April freeze and this
light battering of rain—

a young man approaches us, can
of beer and a Lotto
ticket in his hand. He coos
at the dog: "Little Lassie,"
he says.

I don't know
this boy, he's strange
to the neighborhood. He is
somewhere near twenty,
his clothes are bad, savaged
from his sleep
        and incessant use.

I notice his eyes, seasonless
clouds beneath the innocence
of his unwashed hair.
"Got any
extra change?" he finally asks,
his voice without the
questioning rise, but tight
and flat as if pressed
through a hand guarding his face.
I reach in my wallet and give the boy
everything, the way
I would give to my son:

154

homeless once, without
work or esteem, lonely in that
East Bay shelter for the
one true life that could fit
with him; and how he told no one
until he came to me
and I took him in.

CATCHING THE LIGHT

Susan Clayton-Goldner

At six, my daughter believed stars
could punch holes through the darkness.
For that fleeting second
when each new light stood still
she'd leap to catch it—
hold it briefly in the palms of her hands
like a firefly.

Two years later, the sky starless
and arranging itself for rain,
she held a shoebox coffin
lined with maple leaves.
Air holes dotted the lid.
I remember the sound as it hit the earth
and the blue Siamese kitten shifted its weight—
settled into leaving.
Unwilling to cover it with dirt,
she held the small shovel
like a crutch beneath her arm.

Today, she visits a friend in prison.
"Thank you for bringing her,"
he mouths to me above an offered hand
she cannot take.
Matching it to her own—pressed flat as a moth
against the clear plastic wall.

Leaving, she pauses in front of the windows
and I feel her heart lift itself up.
She watches his fingers flutter—
catch the fading light—
translucent as shadows through the narrow bars.

Somehow strange to me now,
neither child nor woman,
my hand reaches out to touch her face.

This slow and painful rise into herself
pure and clear
as starlight falling.

WHEN SHE ASKS YOU...

Candice Love

when she asks you about...
the night she was conceived
you will want to say how many times you wished you
could take the night back,
ill-timed and regrettable...
but you won't.
you will tell her that love is long-lasting and perfect
       momentous and immediate
you wouldn't give anything for those shining stars

when she asks you about...
what it was like to be pregnant
you will want to lament the sickness and suffering,
      the whispers and stares
      the times you thought about not having her at all...
but you won't.
you will tell her how beautifully pregnant you were,
how wonderful and precious it was
her growing and moving and kicking inside you
dreaming about her tiny face pressed against your own one day

when she asks you about...
the minute she was born
you will want to admit how she tore your body
the tears you shed, the cries,
but you won't.
you will tell her how perfect she was,
her fingers and toes and wailing cries,
that having her was as natural as a mother's love could be

and she will look at you with awe
that there... there where your middle is was her home...
and there... there where she drank for the first time

were you and she...
she will be awed with unspeakable love
and in her eyes
        in her laughter
you'll know that making her
made you.

THE GIFT

Li-Young Lee

To pull the metal splinter from my palm
my father recited a story in a low voice,
I watched his lovely face and not the blade.
Before the story ended, he'd removed
the iron sliver I thought I'd die from.

I can't remember the tale,
but hear his voice still, a well
of dark water, a prayer.
And I recall his hands,
two measures of tenderness
he laid against my face,
the flames of discipline
he raised above my head.

Had you entered that afternoon
you would have thought you saw a man
planting something in a boy's palm,
a silver tear, a tiny flame.
Had you followed that boy
you would have arrived here,
where I bend over my wife's right hand.

Look how I shave her thumbnail down
so carefully she feels no pain.
Watch as I lift the splinter out.
I was seven when my father
took my hand like this,
and I did not hold that shard
between my fingers and think,
Metal that will bury me,
christen it Little Assassin,
Ore Going Deep for My Heart.

And I did not lift up my wound and cry,
Death visited here!
I did what a child does
when he's given something to keep.
I kissed my father.

THE MEMORY OF GRACE AT MR. FONTAYNE'S DOUGHNUT SHOP

James Michael Robbins

If you were a very young child
who perhaps did not eat much
and whose parents may have worried about that,
after your father took your mother to work
he might whisk you away to Mr. Fontayne's doughnut shop
before he dropped you off at the nursery
and went to work himself.

At Mr. Fontayne's doughnut shop
could be every conceivable doughnut,
and Mr. Fontayne himself
must bring the doughnuts to you
that your father hoped
would stretch your little stomach
so you would eat more at home.

And then perhaps your father would lean over
to scribble a word or two on a napkin
for the deaf man who could not speak
but still might sit every morning
in Mr. Fontayne's doughnut shop
with coffee and cigarette,
little and alone,
who might nod or scribble something back
in a sacred silence
that belied the indefinite
in every single moment.

Years after your mother dies
quite possibly in your father's arms
regardless of all the words that could have been said,
and you, perhaps, have moved away,
you might remember those doughnuts

and Mr. Fontayne and the deaf man
and your father
leaning over to do everything he possibly could.
And you may find it is understood
that at such moments
sound has no meaning.

You feel a sudden hollow silence.
You bow humbly over your doughnut.

BATHING MOTHER

Mary Ann Wehler

She sits on a chair to disrobe.
Her breasts slide into her stomach
while it folds over her pubis
like a closed window drape.

I lead her into the shower.
Free of shyness, she allows
me to lift her leg as if
it were a separate

entity. She holds the safety
bar. Her concentration
helps me raise the rest
of her body into the tub.

She rests on the bath stool.
I wash her back, neck, legs;
kneel to gently sponge
her ankles and feet. They

glisten with shiny taut skin.
Mother rules from her seat.
Give me the cloth, please,
hand me the soap. She

washes her breasts, nods
for help, so she can stand
to wash her genitals. Her
spirit still flies, her fractured

vertebrates tie her square
shape to the ground. I lay
in bed that night, remember
after the birth of a child,

being washed by the nurse.
I think of women past,
who washed their dead,
the rituals of life.

SICKNESS AND HEALING

AGNOSTIC AND SON

Michael Cleary

As I boost him on the chair,
my students get interested—in him,
his bandaged hand, even me, teacher
turned father before their eyes.
The hand bigger than Popeye's
fist, but not funny. Under gauze
and ointment, the palm scraped
past flesh and bleeding, fingers
swollen and burst like sausages.

I go on as if he weren't there.

I could explain, but what would I say?
He's stubborn and stupid and five years old,
and the god of escalators didn't care.
But he's a good boy, trying hard
to play with the toy I let him bring.
He shifts in the chair, all his body
moving low, the pain that rode him
through the night familiar now
in a world so awfully changed, so
wickedly strange the hand

forgets, fumbles, the wound
rubbed rough. His face tightens.
His good hand—
its name there waiting in my head—
his good hand reaches out for the bad,
cradles it, lays it down
like a precious thing. Then a deep,
filling breath, an effort to swallow

the pain. I look away, notice the girl

who turns and wipes here eyes, smudges
blotching her perfect cheeks.

Already the moment is blessed forever.
His deep breath, her quiet tears—
courage and compassion
the only sacraments I know.
The holy silence of pain,
the wordlessness of love,
the ungodly tenderness of the world.

MY SON TELEPHONES

Elizabeth Notter

The doctor tells you something is wrong.
The platelets in your blood, the doctor says.
Come back, more tests, a specialist, he says.
At the library, I review the possibilities
and in a minute, or a lifetime, I have watched
you die. I arrange a service
where I tell the ghost

of you how much we loved you but forgot to say.
I remind you how well you did though young
and insecure—always better than you believed.
Your legacy, I told you, is glorious,
those two children, small but strong,
puzzled because you are not sitting
in the church beside them.

I am terrified that I will make this so by thinking it,
am ready to fall over a cliff I built
from no material but fear. I know, finally,
I will drop into the trench where the atheist
finds God and pray, barter, beg.

SICK CHILD

Tim Giles

Though clear skies persist,
a certain gloom begins
to tinge each day,
only a slight
shift in disposition
indicating the more subtle
change, as perceptible as
barometric pressure.
Then illness arrives like a winter storm,
stuffy clouds rolling
like a quilt from horizon to horizon.

Perhaps a glacier is unleashed in her head and chest,
or her body becomes a wind tunnel
filled with a bitter sleet
as she recoils from nourishment.

I always wind up in the rocking chair,
holding her and rocking,
rocking,
amazed by and afraid of how a little one
can rage with such dramatic heat
as I stare out the window,
as if I can will a change in the weather.

And our lives are
frozen
as if paralyzed by snow falling softly, deeply,
catching us unprepared,
dashing to stores in the middle of the night,
murmuring dazedly over the telephone
to employers, doctors, friends,
"Our child is sick…"

THE GREEN SHIRT

Sharon Olds

For a week after he breaks his elbow
we don't think about giving him a bath,
we think about bones twisted like white
saplings in a tornado, tendons
twined around each other like the snakes on the
healer's caduceus. We think about fractures and
pain, most of the time we think about pain,
and our boy with his pale set face goes
around the house in that green shirt
as if it were his skin, the alligator on it with
wide jaws like the ones pain has
clamped on his elbow, fine joint that
used to be thin and elegant as
something made with Tinkertoy, then it
swelled to a hard black anvil,
finally we could slip the sleeve over,
and by then our boy was smelling like something
taken from the back of the icebox and
put on the back of the stove. So we stripped him and
slipped him into the tub, he looked so
naked without the sling, just a boy
holding his arm with the other hand as you'd
help an old geezer across the street, and
then it hit us, the man and woman by the
side of the tub, the people who had made him,
then the week passed before our eyes
as the grease slid off him—
the smash, the screaming, the fear he had crushed his
growth-joint, the fear as he lost all the
feeling in two fingers, the blood
pooled in ugly uneven streaks
under the skin in his forearm and then he
lost all the use of the whole hand,

and they said he would probably sometime be back to normal,
sometime, probably, this boy with the long fingers of a surgeon,
this duck sitting in the water with his L-shaped
purple wing in his other hand.
Our eyes fill, we cannot look at each other,
we watch him carefully and kindly soap the damaged arm,
he was given to us perfect, we had sworn no harm
would come to him.

DAYS OF LOVE

Mark Saba

After the late rain, the cool sun,
the chill and elusive clarity of sky,
he fell asleep in mid-afternoon, when all our intentions

had left us, and the feeling that remained
was one of utter complacency, acceptance, a relishing
of what had been offered us. The weather cells outside

ceased their eternal rhythm, while I carried the quiet
with a book. There may never be days again like this:
accidental, unguided, a father relinquishing every responsibility

except to his croup-stricken son. The world would not have it so.
I felt my old deathbed on the other side of the moment;
questioning religion, and whether I've measured up,

I'll go blindly: All will be lost to these
days of love; and nothing else will have made sense,
nor score, but a time that was known as pure.

WAITING

Maude G. Meehan

The nurse
marks an appointment.
It is my daughter's name
she writes. Once more
the bow is drawn
the arrow aimed
at one of mine.
I wait for word.
The surgeon's verdict
finds its target
in my child;
it pierces me.
I cannot come to terms,
make peace with possibilities
that fracture reason.
I leave the house, go out
into the windswept day, bitter
to see the rainlashed trees
lose early blossoms.
Pacing the cliffs
I sense erosion
as wave on wave
sucks at the shore.

Along the far horizon, storm clouds
squat gray and swollen, waiting.

THRICE ELIZABETH

Marlene S. Veach

She lies beneath
the searching eyes
of the X-ray,
her waterfall of pale hair
spreading about her face
like a burst of sun
in the dark room.

Perhaps she'll live to be
like the Elizabeth I see
now leaving the doctor's office,
spider-splayed,
tapping her cane like
an extra leg as
her daughter pops
a chocolate kiss
in her gaping mouth
to raise her sugar
for the walk to the car.

Then my fair pride
might live to
broken teeth,
distorted limbs
from which youth
and grace have flown.
And she'll come tapping
out from the doctor's
where they've stayed death
for another wink of God's eye.

And her daughter will pop
a sweet into her mouth,
for that extra burst

to make the car where
the smallest Elizabeth
sits in her car seat,
clapping pink hands that
Grandmother is smiling.

Perhaps remembering
the soft trap
of her own car seat
in a half-forgotten memory.
Or lying like a burst of sun
in a dark room where X-ray eyes
see only present tense.
Never know how long
the corridor will be
from a dim room
to the shining future.
Or who might see
this car seat Elizabeth
tap out from a doctor's
office one day.

DECIBELS

Rochelle Natt

As the line graph dips lower, lower,
I, the mother, understand clichés
such as the heart plunges.
"Nerve loss," the doctor calls it.
How many decibels of loss since June?

My son watches through the glass window of the booth.
He looks the same as always—large brown eyes,
brown curly hair, except
for the black headphones.

The walls swim in blue.
I am drowning.
Sound rises in bubbles
as if from the mouth of a fish.
What is the doctor saying?
He speaks of loss again—
mine, my son's.
Not his. I pay at the desk.

The receptionist says,
"Your son must not see you cry."
I didn't know I was crying.
I imagined the sea rolling towards my eyes,
the salt, the brine into my throat.

In the car, my son says, "How did this happen? Why?"

I can't answer. Was it something I did?
A cigarette, a glass of wine
while his cells were still dividing in my sea?
No one can tell me
whether the loss will go deeper,

taking away the banter of friends,
the horn of the oncoming car.
How will I have the courage
to let him cross the street?

My son,
if the tide rises,
I will swim towards you.
I will thrash at the walls of water.
I will bring sound to you.

CAMPING OUT

Robin L. Smith-Johnson

In the log cabin, mid-May,
we fashioned a bed for you.
The doctor had cautioned us
to keep you quiet.
It had been nights of vaporizers,
cough medicine, thermometers.
As if you were an eggshell,
we lifted you onto the mattress
and waited through the night,
listening to you gasp for breath.
Come morning, you woke us.

Mommy, Daddy, quick.
A deer in a clearing, so close.
Then blink, she was gone.
All those elusive bits:
the walk up a small mountain,
you on Daddy's back, bouncing.
I struggled behind, seven months
along, clumsily sidestepping
fallen rocks and branches.

We stopped in a meadow
fragrant with the green haze
of growing things.
There, under the spring sun,
we found bones
of another deer. You were curious,
wanting to touch but we held you.
Some stiffened fur remained,
blood-flecked.

All fades now. It is December
and a new baby sleeps
in the crib in our room.
It is the sound of your cough
that drags me awake.

I stand alone in the dark.
My feet are cold on the bare floor.
I can hear your tiny breaths
coming, then going.
Each breath is a prayer
in the graying dawn.

ALL DAY AT 30 DEGREES

Dixie Partridge

"The melting and freezing points of a substance are the same."
                    —my daughter's science class notes

Still white out.
It can go either way—
like that rim before tears,
like her silence:

> my 17–year daughter runs
> in all weather, skipping meals
> to grow lean.

> We've repeated the ritual:
>   *Dinner's almost on...*
>   *Later, Mom...*
> the closing of the front door.

***

There's a point of exertion
when one more movement will bring a dew
to the brow.
The moving beauty of water
curved above the cup's lip
spills down all sides
with one more drop.

> Last night I looked up the word
> *anorexia,* found it comes from the Greek
> meaning *without reaching out.*

> Now with a feline caution
> I follow her outside, but don't know
> what to call after her,
> her two-mile route into blue light.

***

Not yet a syllable from the eaves
to start the windows singing.
Under the far albino sun,
blue stones of creekbeds
are open mouths in the snow.

Her tall, thin form,
her pale skin and hair,
dissolve into a milky distance.

ON A YOUNG MAN'S BREAK

Naomi Ruth Lowinsky

his mother made this
cable stitch blue
sweater
to match his eyes
when he was five
he was a wandering wooded boy
and there are those among his people wondering
was this thing reaching for him even then behind the blue spruce
below the sunstruck snowpeak in the photograph

they say that he was soft and inward
surrounded by a tender tumbling light his mother wondered what
pulled him down into the hollows of his body
into the corners of the house
was he just going through the motions of becoming

six

nine

bar mitzvah at thirteen his people saw
determination in his torah portion though he lay
among his sweaty socks too many days
there was that time he organized the democratic precincts
they thought they saw a future for him

then why
deep into his twenties
was he still hiding
in the corners of the house
no one had foreseen the day
his sacred horses bolted
he spoke of splintered neon flashing lights

and a leering gang of blue flame goblins
night poured into day
the cooking vessels of his mother
mixed the blood
and milk
no one could comprehend the order
by which he was chosen
a first born mother's son
sweet blue eyed wandering one

where is the voice out of the mountain
to intervene in this?

who is this jackal god who feeds on human brains?

his mother takes his photograph and puts it on the shelf
and in a voice unraveling at the edges of her nerve she says once more
she made this
cable stitch blue
sweater
to match his eyes
when he was five

IN SYMPATHY, MY DAUGHTER SLEEPS BESIDE ME

Paulette Roeske

The laser did not address her flesh
and after all it's a small affair,
the offending part an insult
vaporized by a beam of light.
When they wheel me back to the room,
only a single needle in my hand
feeds its sleepy solution
in a prudent drip. What's so frightening
about that? But understand
my daughter's been waiting
and she's at that sensitive age
between wanting a mother
and wishing her lost in a country
with an unpronounceable name.

Once we are alone,
I watch her face abandon scorn.
When need creeps in,
I invite her to lie beside me
in the narrow hospital bed
and sleep compels us both
into its realm, each for our own
reasons. Sleep, a woman
in a white dress, kind, omniscient,
who has known us forever,
synchronizes our breath—mother and daughter,
wounded and well, touched
by the same falling light,
taking in the same air.
On the single pillow as we sleep

the blond strands of her long hair
travel of their own accord
toward the dark nest of my dark hair,
and her fingers drift
into the palm of my good hand.

SITTING IN A CONCRETE PARKING GARAGE

Greg Kosmicki

at lunch time to eat some raviolis out of a plastic container
that one time held sour cream
or what passes nowadays for sour cream,

I see the grain of the plywood the workers
used to make their forms
when they poured this thick wall in front of me,

and I see on the post that supports the ceiling
some numbers written in pencil
probably too by one of the workers

when they constructed this garage
and the numbers written on the post
make me think of my father

as numbers penciled in on any piece of construction always do,
for as a child I watched him work, hanging sheet rock
nailing studs together, framing, building

something permanent, as I have never bothered
to learn how to do, and I remember the magic,
that he could take out his pencil and make numbers

that would eventually be boarded in and not seen forever,
and the power, too, that went with being one
with permission to write things down on places

where it was forbidden for me to do so.
Now, nearly forty years later, I am sitting in a car in a concrete garage
close, I hope, to the middle of my life

while he nears the end of his
with one thing after the other going wrong
like an old house you work on

but never can finish, because when you get one thing done
two more things fall apart. But when they do
and it's your body, you can't open it up

tear off an old set of lungs like cupboards
from the kitchen wall, knock the skin open like plaster,
find the secret calculations someone left there

that explain how they reached this exact configuration,
how many yards of arteries, the exact spacings of the bones like studs,
the number of feet of capillaries, calculated by hand

with a rectangular yellow pencil,
when your body was new construction,
all the work done on it, still known by heart.

CHEMOTHERAPY

Liz Abrams-Morley

The diminutive chestnut planted
at August's end has quickly grown

bare, its spare skeleton
forewarning of winter.

How can anything so simple—
a child's line drawing,

an icon of a tree—how
can it be that this

will bloom and blaze
in another season?

Brittle and bald,
my mother leans only

slightly as we walk to
her chosen recliner where

she receives her injections
of bright and pastel poisons.

Her hair puffs now in clumps
on her pillow each morning.

The round outline of her skull
is clean and natural as a bare,

cold tree. A new born, she
is defoliated, uprooted.

She watches each silver
shaft fall gently from her,

takes each needle on faith,
believing in another season.

MY MOTHER'S STROKE

Kelly Cherry

Your right eye goes blank,
Can't see even the dark.
The dog barks, and you hear
No bark.

Messages your brain sends
Down your left side, derailed,
Never get where they're going.
And the slow slide

Of your whole brain
Is like that of that train
To Southend—
Went straight off at the bend,
        didn't it,

And into the lake.
But you can still make
The odd, small gesture,
That thought-out investiture

Of movement with sense,
And in your mind, you dance
Under the lake. The puff-fish
        the pancake,
Even the devilfish, trailing his
        whispery wake

Nod and bow
As you waltz underwater.
The music bubbles to the surface
        and me,
Your wondering, admiring, loving,
        listening daughter.

CLIMBING THE MOUNTAIN IN COURAGE

Margaret Robison

When the incline became too steep
my son turned my wheelchair around and dragged it.
His wife walked behind to catch me
in case I lost my balance. My son, tall and bearded,
chose to bring me there for my first outing
from months in the hospital after my stroke,
dragged my wheelchair over the grass, dragged it
over stones to a large, flat rock, on which he parked it,
locked the brakes. Then stood beside me, with his wife,
our pasts spread out in the valley below us.
Houses we'd lived in during difficult years.
His father drinking, me depressed. Hospitals. Schools.
Woods he'd hiked in with his dog. Trees he'd loved.
And stones. His wife's childhood home.
There, on that rock, we could see
the Connecticut River twisting its way through the valley, farmland
green with the harvest of summer, the life
of my grandson already beginning
in the hearts of my son and his wife. My speech
coming back word by word from a shattered language,
sun like sparks on the rippled water.

AFTERMATH

Dixie Partridge

"And God was there like an island I had not rowed to."
                                                    —Anne Sexton

The day gauzed in fog,
I raise my small son from asphalt
like a sacrifice in my arms, his skull,
his shoulders oozing crimson like oil.
My body throbs a strange energy
I think is enough to cast light
through shadow. But I am deluded.

The white fog tastes of tar,
I must empty my arms
to the pallid green gowns. Empty,
empty at the corridor,
my pounding will powerless
in its tremendous force,
and from some depth
the smooth face of fear
rising, rising—
I buckle. My mouth, barren
and open, cannot speak even to Him
in that green place where he waits.

But listen: He comes.
I touch the abraded
flesh, mark of the tire
on his shoulder: my son cries
his pain, and we row
toward home.

CANOEING AT NIGHT WITH MY DAUGHTER ON THE BAY

David Sten Herrstrom

Night is thinner on water.
We can see past the darkness
across the plain to the island we're headed for,
while lights blink on the high, distant bridge like visitors.

We paddle on the same side in unison
so quietly we can almost hear the lights
and, at last, balance each other,
knowing that neither could save the other.

We slide by an island, wooded to the water.
The trees stir, and their foliage changes slowly beside us
into thousands of roosting pelicans.
One ruffles its wings and startles the air above us.
The entire island is uneasy.

Ahead of me her hair
lifts and falls to the rhythm of paddling.
I follow her lead and can no longer hear the sound of disease,
her archipelago of cells now still.

On the island across the plain, we'll build a bonfire
like a lighthouse from the only wood we could find
—some chairs sacrificed—
to celebrate the silence of her body.

Ten yards from the channel, shallows slow us.
Incredulously, we step into the middle of the bay.
From the bridge a watchman looks out of his cubicle of light
to see us walking on water.

We remind each other that gators hate salt
and shuffle our feet to warn the stingrays,
whose wings sound the blackness below us,
remind ourselves that we can cross over.
Together, we are passing to an island we can see.

Returned to the rhythm of the pull,
we aim the boat like an agreement
between us come without a word after long struggle.
She bends to the work in front of me, always ahead of me

as our prow soundlessly plows the island sand,
balancing as she has throughout two-year's passage
—the whistle above, the barbed ripple below—
traveling the plain
her hand dangling in the warm bay, leaving a trail of light.

DISCOVERIES

IN THE EARLY DAYS OF THE WAR

Elisavietta Ritchie

My father beams at me from England.
Behind him, trees, and a tower, squared.
The top, I imagine, must be bombed off:
in Philadelphia our church is spired.

He will soon move on to the front.
His well-pressed uniform will get
dusty, bloody, torn. Aged eight,
an ocean away, I read headlines.

At nineteen I visit an exquisite
English lady among her beds
of rosemary, savory, lavender
drawing ten species of bees.

On her bureau stands the duplicate
of the black-and-white photo on mine.
"I used my last film on him," she sighs.
Her husband off in India, Malaya, Burma,

she billeted officers in her house, she had
plenty of space. "And," he later tells me
but not my mother, "sympathy." He smiles.
I did not know to judge then, won't now.

LESSON ONE: AWARENESS

Susan Spilecki

My mother has eyes
In the back of her head. So have I.
But hers are green, for seeing
Children in torn jeans about to fall
From leafy tree forts;
Zucchini from the icebox corner
Past its crisp kelly prime;
Pine-hued school socks slithering
Down the sleeves of hot-from-the-dryer
Flannel shirts. She sees
What she needs to know.

My city blue eyes,
Like the domed sky caught between towers
Of sooty concrete, show me
A man shuffling along behind;
A police call-box
At the corner, with its dim blue light;
My shoes tightly-laced, hard-
Toed for kicking, soft-soled for running.
Lesson Number One is awareness:
The best warrior
Sees, and avoids the fight.

NORTHERN LIGHT

William Reichard

Midnight and my mother walks
into the room where I sleep
with the blue glow of the television.

She's just come off the evening shift
at the printing factory and small clots
of shaved paper cling to her clothes,

her ink-stained fingers.
She nudges me awake, her face
illuminated by the glowing end

of a cigarette. "Come outside," she says,
her eyes too animated for the late hour;
I obey, though I drag a blanket,

remnant of my sleep, behind me.
Late autumn cuts into my feet
as I walk onto the cement steps

and my mother points into the air
where the sky is alive with fire.
Color braids up in a wild cone

undulating, and light spills red,
green, blue, white
into the unaccustomed night.

"Northern lights," my mother says
and I am amazed as the factory drains
a little from her face, and I realize,

at this hour, in this strange light,
that it is almost possible
to believe in anything.

PERSPECTIVE

Barbara Crooker

Lying on our backs
my baby and I
watch the fall leaves
fly through the air:
like golden finches,
they swoop and glide.
Trees meet above us
in turrets and towers;
a mobile of branches
catches the light;
a kaleidoscope of color
has fallen around us;
we are showered in gold,
coined and minted.

Look, through your eyes
I see
a carousel world
of magic and light.

MY DAUGHTER'S EYES

Andrea Potos

I am watching the evolution
of your eyes, the molten silver
like orbs of hematite your arrived with,
radiating slivers of amber now appearing—
the gold brown of generations—

they widen like sunrise
as your cousin blows at her birthday candles,
small flames flare
and blue sparks crackle
as you watch the lights
that won't extinguish.
I see with you
as if seeing
the dawn of the first fire.

FIRST WORDS

Joan I. Siegel

The way the words push through your lips
sometimes makes me think of the birth of a foal
who squeezes through the dark
a little misshapen and folded
trying to stand on wobbly legs and shake
himself open.

Sometimes you make me think
of a fish feeding on water as you suck in a breath
and out come words like bubbles floating up to the air.

Sometimes you make me think of a glassblower
with his puffy cheeks and eyes squeezed almost shut
intent on the shape turning in the flame.

Sometimes you make me think of a magician
pulling a dove from his sleeve the way you say
bird and it seems to unfold its wings at your mouth
and fly up to a branch on the apple tree.

TEETH

Rebecca Baggett

Bite, you say.
Your four teeth flash,
bright as new-minted
pennies, the unexpected
white of ponies
prancing through
poppy fields. *Bite.*
And you bite
your own hands, laughing,
then cry betrayal,
displaying small fingers
ringed with teeth marks.

The world spreads feasts
before you. Expecting
benevolence, you crunch
geranium leaves, marigold
blossoms, marble-hard
cherry tomatoes, ignoring
my call, from five feet
away: *No, no. Not ripe.*
Bitterness shocks
you like pain or anger;
your flower-face crumples
toward tears.

I thought myself hardened
to beauty's betrayals,
but watching I know
myself vulnerable
to the bright world
once again. Emma,

I want to give you
the world to eat.
Emma, I want to promise
that it will always
be sweet.

DANIEL AND THE DUST

Norbert Krapf

As morning rush hour traffic
cascades past the front

of this old tenant house
toward New York City

he kneels a few feet
in front of the television

head turned away from
his favorite program.

As a Vivaldi concerto
for mandolin serenades

the unfolding of plants
beaded with dew

he lifts an upturned
palm toward specs

of dust floating
in sunlight trickling

through bubbled glass
and cups his hands

with a potion
for me to sip.

THE SWIMMER

Constance Egemo

I wake suddenly,
knowing he's there.
My son stands near the door,
his knees flexed, his arms bent.

In my bedroom in moonlight
he floats in the substance
of his dream.

Now he listens with his forehead
as he used to before he was born.
Now he remembers when his only speech
was a soft dance under my belly.

In his sleep he has come searching for me
to witness the secret world he explores,
and I dare not help him
nor bring him back.

Now, slowly, he reaches up
and questions the air with a gesture.
His hands move toward something
only he can see.

His fingers open
and remain outspread
as though he petitions some gift
from darkness.

now he stares at his hand in awe,
silent, motionless in the still night,
and he takes in his breath
deeply, deeply.

In the moonlight his body,
unfinished as egg white,
becomes opaque, straightens,
changes as I watch.

In his chest
the long dream of the world
opens.

And my son,
smiling with dream knowledge,
turns away from me
and walks into another room.

INFANT CARE

Joel Long

Through some invisible tear, the air
screams. A crazy molecule
at the center of your throat sets
the continent in motion like the jewel
eye of a white snake. All the trees
shake, my bones rattle in their drawers.
I've held oceans quieter than you,
little city with your interstates
and steam trains.

You're a pocket of warm weather
stirring in the valley below my ribs.
How many birds do you hold within you?
Whose job was it to carve your wild eyes?
I've been flying with the insects so long
I barely recognize my own kind,
though I understand it is common
to find the familiar so strange.
These clawing hands, they cannot be mine,
and they're not. They're yours.

How complicated continuity is.
You writhe like a cat, strong
in these arms that seek to tame you.

A FATHER'S DISCOVERY

John Sangster

It's not as if at some point
you finish

like the craftsman who steps back
(wiping his hands on his apron)
to view his work: "So, it's done."

Who's to say when you finish?

Maybe never.
Or, at the earliest, much much later
when the roles reverse.

Perhaps it's over
long before you know:
pieces in place
trajectory set.

FIRSTBORN DAUGHTER LEAVING HOME

Mariah Hegarty

Your patchwork baby quilt hangs on the wall
pinned up with tacks, its circumference
too small now to warm your dreams.
An entire history woven in this fabric,
three quarters of a year's patience
waiting for flesh stitching itself
invisibly, cell by cell.

I see myself then, as I knelt, rounded
belly pressing against my thighs.
I matched couples of calico as seriously
as a child playing Old Maid. Each
square paired with its mate—

the peacock ground in this swatch
harmonizing with the red wearing
roses of the same hue. Six blocks
wide, seven long, bordered in shades
of faded denim—hand-pieced. The tracks
of stitches mince in even lines,
connecting the rows. I never doubted

I could sew perfection into the seams
of your life. Now I sit on the floor
of your room in the last of the day's
light and examine my creation. Quilting
binds the top and bottom to the warmth
in the center; I pulled those threads
taut as my unripe cervix,

dividing the squares into segments,
a pie cut into eight neat slices. Now

gaps have appeared in the perpendicular
where straight-edged lines snapped
under the tension—it's give that lends
strength in the end. From across the room
my mistake is obvious. A larger order

is completely absent, lights and darks
juxtaposed at random in no particular
pattern. That row there has all reds
and blues of the same intensity—
maroon flush with navy, alongside
cobalt, next to wine. Unnoticeable
up close, from here the colors blend
in an unbroken strip. So intent, at twenty
on the details, I never stepped back
to see the whole. All these years later
I must remind myself,
it covered you just the same.

FLIGHT PATTERNS

Marjorie Maddox

July 17, 1996

On time, normal, through average air,
your plane came home to me
out of dusk above the Montoursville horizon
and settled without fanfare on the runway
just as, in New York, that other plane took off
to Paris with the neighbors' children
pressing their faces to the window to see
the last of Long Island,
their horizon waiting to explode
into sunset.

We didn't know driving home,
lugging your two suitcases from the car
and up our stairs to the bedroom,
the emptiness of other rooms,
the space on a pillow where a head should be.

Our first child slept soundlessly
in the room of my body.
We had just learned she was there,
the trip we would all take together
as yet unplanned.

What patterns are these?
Prayers for the unborn crisscrossing
those for the newly dead,
a strange radar of dread
hugging hope in the stomach.
Parents of the just-buried and just-begotten
circling a small town with their weeping.

Before I knew,
I slept, exhausted
by the small one within me

curled tight as a tornado
ticking its way to an explosion
I longed for.

Exhausted, too, from your travel,
you didn't sleep, but read
from the doctor's color brochures
our child's beginnings,
the daily care we must take;
then perched yourself
before the black-and-white news
and learned.

When you woke me,
your voice was the sound of small birds
flapping from the nest,
the hush of the watching world
huddled and blazing.

A HIGHER LOVING

Laura Golden Bellotti

It's easy to love your own children
but a higher loving is to love someone else's
as dearly as a mother would her own.

That is what I believed when I was a child
loved so dearly by my mother
and already wondering about being one.

Mothers automatically love their children
because they look and act like them
giving them back themselves in a newer form.

That is what I believed when I was a child
seeing my grown-up self in my mother's gentle eyes
and sexy, self-assured mouth.

I will not need to have my own child
because I will love someone else's
and my love will be stronger
than the automatic love of flesh and blood.

That is what I pledged
in my heart born of my own mother
who taught me to wonder
and to love by loving me.

I didn't know I would fall in love
with my own child before he was born
a child of my love for my lover
a loving born of my mother.

Every child carries our desire to love
as he carries too his own wonder

we pass the loving on to him or her
to father and mother.

It is easy to love my own child
the way I was so gently loved by my mother
but I believe I would love him still
if he were born years from now or long ago
to another.

LEARNING HOW

Sally Croft

Not new the blue two-wheeler, a cousin's
outgrown, but what joy—bikes were scarce
those war years. In the slack hours
between lunch and dinner at our restaurant my father
in white chef's pants and shirt ran behind me
holding the seat as I wobbled
down the sidewalk a lump a rag doll
sitting a headstrong colt
determined to toss me. And would have except for my father's
hand on the seat, righting the bike each time before its swerve
tumbled me off. Nervous, I took quick looks back especially as
balance came, not trusting, believing it was he who kept
the wheel steady. Until checking
I saw his big grin far behind as I rode the bike
solo to the end of the street. As he'd known I would, steadying
me until I knew it too.

JOY AND PLEASURE

POSTPARTUM

Barbara C. Behan

On this night within night
of the blue arctic winter
my house shakes down to sleep.
Night light and slippers
I sink and sigh, too.
O couch, be my lover.

Upstairs, hidden
is a glowing spark sleeping.
She shines
possibility
leaking under the door.

I love her

I miss her

the union we had when
my body contained her.

She plunders me,
wrenches me open.
I am the soft bruisy flesh
of a fruit near its center.

Please someone, somewhere
make up a new language
for the smooth nap of hair
on my lips, for the press
of her kitten-paw fingers, her
tiny clean earthworm
of mouth on my nose.

Write down her notes

which my ears
were made perfect to hear.

TO THE SAME LISTENER

Wyatt Townley

1.

you are my daughter and i am
your mother how do i know
because you swam the length of me

you slipped in one Friday
and swam out shining
with all my insides

i hand you my breasts every hour
what's in me now enters
who you are

my daughter and i your
mother this i know
i wash you off and change

your clothes soaked
with the river that
flows from me to you

and ends up running
back over my hands

2.

while you were sleeping
your lips still suckling
imagined breasts fingers

coiled into questions
they were asking of god
under a blanket of tugboats

your chest rose and rose
into your nightshirt
through the seams of the ceiling

past treetops to a starry nest
where a breath once sailed you
to me and you were born

3.

the color of your eyes
an impossible navy
blue is not from daddy

is not from me
but from the march night
sky you tore

on your first swan dive

4.

joy sweeps your face
as wind enters leaves
your cheeks rushing up
to your eyes in a smashing

smile when suddenly panic
strikes and you are the storm
crossing the orchard mowing
down mom and other trees

in the course of a moment
you are the joy and the agony
grown-ups have buried for centuries
and called it weather

before you learn to lie
what's inside you spins out

across the tiny skyscape
of your face and i will bask

and chill for as long as we can bear it

5.

i speake the queene's english
you jabber in secret

operas sung
in cribs around the world

from paris to soweto
a libretto

forgotten by champions
of spelling bees

6.

you are not my daughter and
i am not your mother we
are just swimmers of

light you teach me
to play with the bright
red hat of the beggar

to hear the commandments
of thunder and the prayers
of a housefly the same

song sailing from the deep
to the same listener

NESTLING

Connie Wasem

Except for the open plains of daylight
after we begin to sleep and are held
captive and in good company,
except for the white bricks
of our small house all the neighbors can see,
we are alone, tugging each other,
while the day smoothes over us like water
and tumbles away from the bed.

We forget the coolness of untouched skin,
we forget the songs the summer wind
thrums through the trees. Our retreat
stirs these layers of lavender sheets—
your pod-like feet tucked in the nook
of my bent hips, your small head
burrowing the plush of my breast.

Even the dogs can't disturb us,
for we have sealed our ears against
the afternoon. Our mouths forget
everything except our warm skin—
tight clams remembering the need
for milky pearls made slowly
of sand no swimmer can reach.

FATHER, YOU ARE ANCIENT

William Dickenson Cohen

Father, you are ancient,
grinning your goofy smile.
One hundred and sixteen times
my age, you are today; yes,
I cannot help but smile
when you make those funny,
complicated sounds.
I wave my tiny arms
and feel your joy
splashing onto me,
your warm breath on my cheeks
and your gentle caress
making my bright eyes brighter.

Father, you are ancient.
I will forget this moment,
only because I cannot help it,
but please, retell it to me
when I am able to remember,
so that I can be reminded
that you loved me always,
Father, ancient
and never more alive.

MAX, AT TWO MONTHS

Julia K. Singer

It's three AM and I'm nursing you back to sleep.
Your soft, sweet hum—
hee-he... hee-he,
and your father's snore
mingle with the dog's labored sighs.

Tonight's sonata has many movements;
the churning of the night train begins
followed by a chorus of crickets
and the cli-
click of the clock.

Yet it's your voice I hear above them all—
your stirring groans,
your catching cry,
your silly dreamer's laugh.
Your voice pulls me out of dreams of ocean swells
and soccer fields.

You
have opened the night for me
like a key to an attic box,
filling my dreams
with sound.

TO MY SON, LAUGHING IN HIS SLEEP

Freya Manfred

Since he was a baby
I have awakened in the night
startled
by the bell-sweet sound
of his laugh.
I am propelled,
cold, knees creaking,
across the cluttered floor
to his bed,
my face above his face:
yes, he is asleep,
and smiling.

Back in my bed I hear again
his high warble.
How I envy this boy
who is not mine,
who was never mine.
How I praise him
for making everything in the world right
for one moment.

TWO A.M. FEEDING

Edith Rylander

Here in our safe bed, in the warm valley
Between his father's back and my nursing body,
Five-week-old Eric drinks the world at my breast.

Outside, whatever the bones of Sioux and settler
Whisper in the dark of two A.M.,
Nothing moves but the easy slip of water,
Snow weeping down, worms quickening in the compost.

How did we earn this? Eric with his soft greed;
Me with the petty guilts and charities
of thirty-two years in a well-fed country.
We have earned nothing. And though I starved myself
Till Eric cried and jerked at the limp nipple,
Those scrawny kids would shiver under bridges,
Or scream when the roof fell in a sheet of fire.
The men with the big boots would still kick doors in.
We have earned nothing. Nobody earns anything.

It will be morning soon, time to fry bacon,
Kiss people, talk about fishing, plan the garden.
The robins are back. The apple tree will flower,
However man suffers, and desires to suffer.

AFTER MAKING LOVE
WE HEAR FOOTSTEPS

Galway Kinnell

For I can snore like a bullhorn
or play loud music
or sit up talking with any reasonably sober Irishman
and Fergus will only sink deeper
into his dreamless sleep, which goes by all in one flash,
but let there be that heavy breathing
or a stifled come-cry anywhere in the house
and he will wrench himself awake
and make for it on the run—as now, we lie together,
after making love, quiet, touching along the length of our bodies,
familiar touch of the long-married,
and he appears—in baseball pajamas, it happens,
the neck opening so small
he has to screw them on, which one day may make him wonder
about the mental capacity of baseball players—
and flops down between us and hugs us and snuggles himself to sleep,
his face gleaming with satisfaction at being this very child.

In the half darkness we look at each other
and smile
and touch arms across his little, startlingly muscled body—
this one whom habit of memory propels to the ground of his making,
sleeper only the mortal sounds can sing awake,
this blessing love gives again into our arms.

IDOLATRY

DC Berry

At St. Paul's Methodist,
at the altar, the kids
gather for the pastor's pep talk—

the boys with clip-on ties,
girls in dresses
like teepees full of white

petticoats. The preacher in his
black robe is the candle
with the red tongue—our kids

his moths that can't be still,
scratching, winking,
yawning, and waving while

we parents worship them,
our eyes big as headlights,
our smiles frozen

crescents. Same kid
we'd threatened with Time Out
Unless you put

your shoes on really QUICK.
Up there,
now, waving like the Pope,

our propeller,
our Mr. Goodwrench, our
Kleenex waver.

We dazzled parents sitting there
like the second coming, though we're
only getting our windshields cleaned.

BACKSCRATCH BOY

James P. Lenfestey

Your righteousness
is mighty as a king's.
Your anger lasts the time
an egg cooks.
Your smile charms cobras
and cataracts.
Your indolence is a jungle
where butterflies live whole lives.

A father is driven mad
before these gifts.

But we can scratch each other's
backs for hours,
like monkeys quiet in the trees
or baboons squatting
in the grass.
Your hands salve
old wounds in my back,
while I find in yours a billion
nerve endings that all shriek joy.

FROG HUNTING

Peter Cooley

Almost always ahead of us,
hippety, in the night,
their sixth sense
radar to pick us up
and give them, hippety,
one jump on us,
the frogs dot the sidewalk
of summer after rain.
They are pursued, hop,
by two little girls,
barefoot, hair loose
in their faces, their hands
hippety, clasped in mine,
tugging this tired father.
Through sidestreets, the puddles
like black marshes, the concrete
buckled and split, hip-
pety, I'm pulled, hop.
But should a tired frog,
hippety, a lazy one,
a dreamer, one fat
with too many flies
or a frogleg-watching stud,
hippety, happen to pause
and feet of a demoiselle or two
land on his clamminess,
then, hippety, hippety, up
the father's legs they jump
to be carried, shrieking,
one in each arm, wriggling,
home to their mother, hop.

AT THE SAWMILL

Anna Viadero

It was the summer
you owned the river:
sawgrass, milkweed, sycamore.
The rumor of deer ran
through one narrow meadow.
Monarchs rushed
from butterfly bush
shook loose by hustling muskrat.

Scooping confederate clay
from the hoary bank,
you sculpted small idols,
painted your bodies muddy,
swirls and arrows
from face to feet,
then stood huddled
into the mother mud
and for a moment seemed
invisible.

Coaxing mica
from the brittle rock face,
stars of time, you
tossed it into the current,
watched it rush
the water red, gold,
turned to me and
crowed wild
as though you'd
pulled down the sun.

BRAIDS

Miriam Pederson

Her hands separate
the strands of her daughter's hair
feeling in its texture
her own childhood summers—
the coolness on her neck
as she ran along the beach,
her braids striking the air.
Every day a grand expectation—
a leaf unfolding before her eyes,
its veins spreading in all directions.
At bedtime her mother released her braids,
brushed her hair
and praised its fullness,
its shining light.

When your mother braids your hair,
you must sit very still.
You will notice things you hadn't before—
a crack in the wall the shape of a teapot,
a scuff mark on your shoe,
the quiet breathing of your mother
as she weaves your hair
into countless indelible summers.

SPRING TRAINING

Wendy Mnookin

Ed Smith Stadium, Sarasota, Florida

Watching from the bleachers, my son and I
finish the last two chocolate donuts
the motel sets out for guests, while under my breath
I instruct the pitcher—much larger
than on TV—to put one over the plate. But
he tosses the ball, hardly a pitch at all, and my son
scribbles "BB" in the program book, baseball code
so much easier for him than sixth grade. At the seventh

inning stretch, they call the number on his ticket
over the loudspeaker—"I told you
it's my lucky day"—and he's out on the field
pitching for pizza. Before he can return
to his seat, the manager taps his shoulder. "You wanna be
bat boy?" My son flashes me one undimmed smile
and doesn't look back for the rest of the game.
He crouches by the bullpen while the batter

warms up. He runs for the bat discarded at the plate,
wipes sweat from his nose with the back of his hand,
every now and then spits
from a wad of gum in the corner of his mouth,
pretends he doesn't
have a mother. But I'm here,
and I see him, hard hat askew,
have everything he wants, and know it.

THE OLD LIFE *(excerpt)*

Donald Hall

There were joys, even
in Connecticut; there were miracles
in the suburbs. Snow
still lay in patches on Ardmore's north side
when the mailman brought
the catalogue—with pages as flimsy
as a comic book's,
four colors printed askew—from the Bliss
Fireworks Company
of East Valparaiso, Indiana.
I became scholar
of smudged images: SPECIAL MAJESTIC
VENETIAN NIGHTS
and GOLDEN ETERNAL SHOWERS OF ECSTASY.
I put checks by Roman candles
and skyrockets that dropped lead
soldiers under tissue
parachutes.
My father printed out
the form in his neat letters.
When the box came I unpacked it
and lined up pinwheels and bombs,
sorting the fountains and green fire.
On the fourth we drove
to a county where fireworks were legal
and parking on a dirt
road after dark flared our paradise
of fire.
The next day
I began right away to plan ahead
for next year, foreseeing
fireworks always with my young father,
slender rockets unpacking

their quick shoots of burning petals,
      green gold, as we two
became one person, ecstatic and joint,
      blossoming together
into smoke that enlarged and expired.

WATCHING DADDY PLAY PINOCHLE

Barbara Brent Brower

The air was as blue and thick
as cows' tongues
as they argued philosophy
drank beer
shouted
pounded the table
laughed

When not shouting pounding howling
laughing or slapping cards down or grabbing them up
or counting piles of money
they were chewing thick sandwiches
with hot mustard on rye

Drinking beer and pounding shouting counting
the air blue with smoke and words chewed and re-chewed
until I fell asleep on Bobeh's prickly couch

I woke up when Uncle Dave yelled

Daddy came to carry me to the car
stubble-faced red-eyed
smelling of beer and garlic and cigarettes
his tongue thick with winning

ROCK N ROLL

Tony Gloeggler

"Don't Be Cruel"
came on the clock radio and mom
knocked on my door,
walked in, dropped an arm
full of laundry
and grabbed my hand. She rolled
shoulders, shook hips,
whirled around me and fell
back on my bed
out of breath and laughing
like a girl
in the front seat of a cadillac
with hot winds
rippling her long black hair

APPLES AND ORANGES

Angela M. Mendez

my mother sits at the table
peeling tangerines for my father
The sweet citrusness of the fruit
cha-chas through the room
like an exotic dancer
rubbing boa feathers under my nose
I want to say
"he isn't doing anything
why can't he peel his own fruit?"
but as she hands him one tangerine
and their eyes meet
it is in that instant
that their love blinds me
and I forget what I was going to say

WEDDING DRESS

Arlene Clayton Eager

One moment we were laughing,
   clowning, playful
Then I said, or she said,
   It must be time.

With upraised arms, slim body swaying,
   she disappeared, the child of mine,
   in a cloud of pure white cotton.
Folds fell, slow-motion, into place.

Behold the bride, no longer child—
   the lovely, honest face,
   the heart so kind.
A simple, dazzling beauty.

This is what it means,
   to take the breath away.
I called across the years,
   a thing I rarely do:

Mama—
   if only you could see her.

NOURISHMENT

Binnie Pasquier

He sat with me
in a kitchen corner
a bowl of steamers
briny vapor
between us
as I pried open each clam
pulled the plump drop
by its resisting foot
holding it out to him
tossing the shell
among the empties
with a clink.

His eyes half-closed
my father savored each one
as a luxury
somehow fallen
into the wrong man's mouth.

ANGER AND GRIEF

WATER WALK

Wendy Mnookin

On the beach children pile sand into castles, racing
to the water to splash and dunk, their suits gaudy
against the lake's shadowed skin. Voices of older
sisters and brothers ring from the rafts—girls
smooth sunscreen onto their perfect bodies,

boys jostle and push. I have just taken off
my thongs and shirt when the whistle blows three times,
"Everyone Out." A child is missing. His name
scratches from a bullhorn, while lifeguards—children themselves,
it seems to me—line up in deep water and dive

on command. I hardly have time to watch their efforts
when I'm led into place for the water walk. I take
the hand of a woman in a lavender swimsuit. Tall
and stout, she bends to the task in silence. I take
the hand of a man, bearded and bony, who swears

if he finds the boy alive, he'll kill him. My eyes
tear against the glare. The water, furred
by wind and churned by our legs, distorts my vision,
so I'm not sure what I see underneath. The surface,
which minutes ago appeared calm, slaps sharply

at my belly and thighs, the temperature strangely cold
for August. Look at us—nine shivering adults
slogging along to search for a child we hope
digs unobserved in some crowded corner of beach.
None of us has the wide eyes of faith I've seen

in paintings of Jesus as he walks on water in a rough
sea. We know the worst may happen, if not
today, then someday, if not to us, then to someone

and still we let our children run with their pails
to the water, we let them shape wet sand and decorate

castles with pebbles, with gray and pink shells, we let them
choose each whorled shell, intricate as the half
moons that shine, small and white, on the finger-
nails of their muddied hands, though at any moment,
distracted, they may disappear.

THE WHITE BOAT

Judith H. Montgomery

There are the white lights lowered over the steel table,
then the white walls sliding past the cart,

the snows banked beyond the narrow window,
the white crumpled tissues balled in pale fists.

The paperwhite narcissus rooted in pebbles and water,
unfolding its fragrance as a salve.

The clear looped tube runs with the milk
of juiced poppies, the ivory mirror turned to the wall.

The blanched fingers of relatives, snapping
open and shut, and shut, the clasp of a purse, a pen.

The august heads conferencing beyond
door 32B, lips pressed tight, bloodstopped.

The delicate limbs laid against white
sheets tugged tight to ward off failure

and the small white bones rising to the surface
of flesh like the bellies of fish in a basket.

*

There was Odysseus smashed free of his raft
on the wine-dark, white-capped sea;

and the white goddess, Leucothea, shifting
the veil from her ivory brow, from the coil

of her hair, from her neck like a swan's,
from the nook of her shoulder, white elbow, wrist.

251

Her white veil cast on the sea, her raft
wrapping him up and away from death.

*

There is the bright struggle against the white cells,
sails bellied and driving the blood tide.

The grape stain of bruises, seaweed rising
to float on the paperwhite skin.

There is the white veil of the sheet drawn
over the boy's body,

the body shining like a light
from the bed, from the bottom of the sea.

SISTER'S DRAWINGS AFTER LITTLE BROTHER'S DEATH, III

Rawdon Tomlinson

Scratched to life
on the white, lined sheet
torn from a notebook:

A storm of zigzags
wave up and down,
spirals and cones erupt
from the center
of the giant obstacle course
without exit—

a stick figure lies on its side
spread-eagle, adrift in white
as an astronaut cut loose in space,
hair pasted flat as a toupee,
black holes for eyes;

another at the bottom
looks up
with zero-howling mouth,
hair streaked from the head like claw marks,
arms held out in space
crucified:

she says, "A dead child
and a lost girl with volcanoes
and whirlwinds."

TO A CHILD, A SPRING POEM

Peter Cooley

Along the boulevards the first camellias
lift their lush fire like flambeaux to the twilight
erect, processional. In the live oak
the mockingbird takes up her shriek again,
and by the black lagoon the dragonfly
assumes, above the timpani of crickets,
its iridescent, slow descent over the lilies.
This is the hour fathers are coming home.
They are crossing the yards, the cold, sallow ground,
bearing children in their arms
as I take you, up to the darkening houses.
And, had you lived, we would be inside now,
snug, out of sight. We would not stand together
holding up this sky night after night,
our backs against the wind—
my words wind and yours not even that
and the stars, the dark stars, an instant, vanishing.

CONVERSATION WITH AN UNBORN CHILD

Peggy Hong

you are the one that wakes me at night
I recognize your small fingered grasp
weightless as dawn

> I could be anything
> fish   bird   stone
> I visit you at the river
> it is dark   it is winter

you are the one whose name
never escapes my lips
is the baby a girl or a boy
I asked the doctor
he scoffed it's not a "baby"

> not a baby I hardly
> matter   mine
> is the space
> between remembering
> and forgetting

you who barely knew me
why me? I bled
in the nurse's arms
all she could offer me was valium
mine was the only cry
in the entire building

> I will leave you
> with what you asked
> to learn

I never asked for this
the masks the heavy blue drapes
the sonogram they would not
allow me to keep
the cramps
that curled me in my narrow futon

                              unravel yourself   it's time
                              to stop asking
                              here is the threshold   yours
                              to cross

no longer locked in my womb

THE LAST STAR

Gail Ghai

My mother is like your mother—she is the satiny night.
Five silver stars spun from her body; four of them fell
to earth. The fifth, the last star, burnt out in the sky.
That was my brother, Brian Neil, the second son
my father sought, named, but incomplete, who came

too early that Christmas Eve when the red blinking of the
 ambulance
outshone the crimson lights on the tree. In the blue cold
 Alberta night,
where the case of Coca Cola froze on the back porch, my
 mother was rushed
to the hospital. Later that night, when he told us, *your mother
 lost the baby,*
my father's voice was strangely soft, his face dazed as a
 startled buck.

He fed us lopsided turkey sandwiches and cold mashed
 potatoes.
Instead of milk, he treated us to fizzy cokes, he shared his
 cashews,
the ones he hid in the garage. When we picked out the
 raisins in
the Christmas cake, he ignored it. Then he opened the box of
 Black
Magic chocolates he'd been saving. After five we all felt better.

For the next six nights the menu was repeated until it was
 depleted.
While he was at work we ate peanuts for breakfast, popcorn
 for lunch.

We developed stomach aches while our hearts ached. But we
     were fun-
centered, self-centered, and we soon forgot our grief, played
     with our new
Monopoly around the clock, not missing the brother we had
     never known.

Our mother returned, thinner than white ribbon trimming
     the tree.
She sat by the gas fire, gazing into the blue cone of the flame.
She smoked, smoked, smoked. Her haze and her hush filling
     up the house
though my asthmatic brother begged her to stop; while my
     sisters and I
pleaded for her to speak our names. But she stayed silver cold,
     silent as a star.

OUR LADY OF THE SNOWS

Robert Hass

In white,
the unpainted statue of the young girl
on the side altar
made the quality of mercy seem scrupulous and calm.

When my mother was in a hospital drying out,
or drinking at a pace that would put her there soon,
I would slip in the side door,
light an aromatic candle
and bargain for us both.
Or else I'd stare into the day-moon of that face
and, if I concentrated, fly.

Come down! come down!
she'd call, because I was so high.

Though mostly when I think of myself
at that age, I am standing at my older brother's closet
studying the shirts,
convinced that I could be absolutely transformed
by something I could borrow.
And the days churned by,
navigable sorrow.

BREAKFAST WITH MY FATHER

Deborah Casillas

In winter our morning lives took on ritual,
in the dark dripping valley dawn when
my feet froze on the floor, when we
moved through the house like ghosts
in the dim light, as if a voice might shake
from us the fragile bond we shared
at the beginning of each day. The metal
stresses of the heater warming up
like bones rattling in a box, the rustling
of bread in a cellophane bag, the soft slide
of a toaster going down. No words
cut the pretense of completion: the sound
of two voices would remind us
of the absent third. This was the steady time,
our unvarying breakfast, sweet smell
of my father's tea, smoke from his blackened
toast curling from the toaster. We ate
in the kitchen side by side, I perched
like a cat on the metal stool and he
standing stooped beside me at the counter.
Silence linked us, an austere anchor
before we went our ways. Our lives bereft,
bone-bare, I felt loss wrap around me
like the smoke from my father's cigarette.

IN THE CLERESTORY OF LEAVES

Barbara Crooker

We drive to your special education preschool
under an arch of maples, half green, half turned to gold,
the dark branches bold as the ribs
of a great cathedral, flying buttresses
that bend the light.
You haven't changed in the last two years,
developmentally delayed, mildly retarded,
school a struggle to stay in your seat,
say the beginnings of words,
point to colors and shapes.
While you wrestle with scissors,
daub with paste, I sit in the hallway,
trying to write, turn straw into gold.

When our two hours are spent,
we drive back up the hill toward home,
see the stand of mixed hardwoods
in full conflagration: red-gold, burnt orange,
blazing against the cobalt sky.
The architect who made these trees
was sleeping when he made this boy.
And my heart, like the leaves, burns & burns.

DOING HOMEWORK WITH A LEARNING DISABLED CHILD

Ginnie Goulet Gavrin

For my son,
somewhere in the synapses
the connection is broken.
Splitting his intelligence
into fractions. Making letters
jam together on a page. Words
float away from each sentence.

For my son,
shut behind the ancient oak door
of his classroom,
squirming in his seat
as though shaking loose
those missing words that hide,
lost where the impulses
missed their cue, lost
in the microscopic spaces
where language meets meaning.

For my son,
who is commended for his effort
but not for the product.
For whom progress
is usually measured
by mistakes eliminated.

For my son,
whose paintings never grace
the classroom walls,
whose recess is spent in
tutoring, catching up, making do.

For my son,
whose letters scratch
the paper full of holes,
who misreads the directions,
but works on diligently
like an athlete
running for the wrong goal.

For my son,
who saves his tantrums
of frustration for me.
I receive them
without grace, patience
worn thin as a membrane
he can see through.

Leaning over the kitchen table
we arrive at the right answers,
late, and out of breath.
Past bedtime, past caring
we tuck pencils and papers away
and let the quiet dark of night
draw its slow bead of sleep
over all his hard work.

A BALDING FATHER

John Gray

His was a lonely life-time fight
against hair-loss.
We competed all our lives
with the face bent into the mirror,
the wad of hairs protruding through
the sad slits in the comb.
It was not the ones who had
come from his seed
who defined his middle years,
that would stick to his
every movement, even watch
his boring games of golf
from the cart path or sit beside
him for hours lake-side,
long before he trusted us
with a fishing pole.
His eye was always on what he
was shedding, the cold evidence
growing grayer by the year
or the bald patch, spreading like
a cancer that wouldn't even guarantee
a suitable departure from this world
when it peaked.
In a way, we could have been
that bald spot, our growing
shrinking him into a corner,
the years our bones added to
their fledgling marrow sucked away
from what he had left.
But he chose less animated evidence
for what was happening to him,
what wouldn't stop,
what couldn't be prevented with all

the phony restorers in America.
He could have held us, kissed us,
passed on the things he knows,
ennobled the aging process.
But even now, bald as the proverbial
billiard ball, if he notices us at all,
it's to watch our hair like a hawk,
waiting for signs
of the first mutinous follicle
or extra inch of forehead,
as if his only hope for hair these days
is whatever it is we lose.

DADDY

Sharon Scholl

You are the emptiness
I carried like a sack,
the vacancy I wore
like Catholic penance.

The uncles I once stuffed
into that hole
were sucked into splinters
by that depth of need.

Grandfathers coaxed
from rocking chairs
could not nail shut
the black shaft of my loss.

My dolls had dads
who came from work
with waiting laps, arms full
of hugs and story books.

But I had cracking photographs,
yellowed Christmas cards,
persistent wisps of memory,
the solace of my fantasies.

Daddy, time-thief; daddy, dream-snatcher,
daddy of the power of absence,
forgiveness is irrelevant;
I have lived over you.

ELEGY FOR MY FATHER

Sylvia Ryan

I'll tell you how I'd like to remember you:
You toss me in the air and always catch me;
You hold my hand along the darkening street;
Your smile says their words can never harm me.
But none of this occurred. For what memories
Could be left of you, who turned to ash when I
Was just learning to name you? Neither the key
To a dusty forbidden trunk nor snapshots found
Scattered in the back of a drawer one autumn give
Much yield. In one, the only evidence
Of us, you hold my newness for a lifetime.
Only in dreams are you real: You lean against
A sea wall. You look straight at me. I strain
For a sign. Behind you a whole ocean is silent.

CUTTINGS

Jane Butkin Roth

Your home
never hinted of four children;
their toys, books, stains, tantrums
conspicuously absent. You,
resplendent in your gown,
green silk with roses.

As cuttings from your garden
hovered obediently in Waterford
next to coffee table books
arranged in perfect lines,

we cooed and fussed over
your latest Christian Dior baby
when Elsa pranced in,
showing off her new self-styled, a three-year-old's
self-inflicted hair-do,
now jagged remnants
of Alice-in-Wonderland locks.

You grabbed what hair was left
and forced her, prisoner,
to the antique Italian mirror.
Snapping spirit and neck, you screamed,
Look how ugly you are!

As I heard the voice and felt
the hard hand on your daughter,
I witnessed—I became
the tragedy of Elsa, felt
her back hunched, aged and shrunken,
and I knew
it didn't matter what came after.
Apology or forgiveness or how many years.

She would never
hold her head the same, never
be so filled with
herself,
never dance
the way she graced me with her movement.

REMORSE

Joan I. Siegel

My sudden anger darkens your face
and you pull back as though pricked
by thorns in the honeysuckle. You
look at me amazed. For the moment
there is nothing else.
Then we suck in our breath.
Blood rises under your cheeks.
Tears drop from your eyes.
They fall one by one
onto my hands, burning
my skin.

MY DAUGHTER'S ANGER

Rebecca Baggett

When her face contorts with rage,
when she shrieks, insisting
that she will not she will never
we can never never make her,
I remember my father's rage and how
it erupted, suddenly, unpredictably,
while we all froze, listening,
like wild things waiting for the predator
to pass or not to pass us by.
Gripping my daughter's arms, I think
of my own anger, the anger I cannot measure
because I never let myself feel it,
because I knew even at five or six
that anger was never safe. I think
of that thin dark river streaming
through my body for twenty-five years,
until it fed her, growing in me, fed her
an anger that will not be silenced,
will not yield. Staring at my daughter's
face, I imagine myself cheated again
of my anger, forced to mother hers,
imagine that this, too, is mine, that she
will voice it for me, and I am afraid
for her and glad.

TEARS FOR A DAUGHTER

Linda Tanner Ardison

Each day, I labor with you new;
My paper heart rips like thin
Tissue on the fragile gift
Of all my hopes for you.
I have no anesthetic ease
For this delivery, no breathing
Technique mastered years
Before you entered life.
From that first flutter-kick
Within my vast, protective ocean,
You slid to this darkened, adolescent
Air, and now I long to toughen us,
Create a carapace around the fears
That bloom exquisitely each evening,
Leaving blood stains on the day.
Our sudden separateness erupts;
I want to steal you back to me,
My changeling, my invited love.

LOST AND FOUND

CB Follett

My daughter has found her birth mother.
Soft rocks the cradle.

Hard-scrabble, this search,
this last search, begun in her gut
somewhere around eight.

Loss colored all her stables.
Rejection rode the winning horse,
balked at the fences, and threw her
in the mud. Again and again.

One day, she got an answer. Hired
a detective, who took her clues
to the head of the line, and so
she sent a letter. Got one back,
and some pictures. Now at last,
she looks like someone,
is somebody's daughter.

And I wish her
the joy of it, as she rises
out of the mysterious density of loss,
and I fall toward it.

LULLABY FOR 17

Linda Pastan

You are so young
you heal as you weep
and your tears
instead of scalding
your face like mine
absolve
simply as rain.

I tried to teach you
what I knew: how men
in their sudden beauty
are more dangerous,
how love refracting light
can burn the hand, how memory
is a scorpion

and stings with its tail.
You knew my catechism
but never believed. Now
you look upon pain
as a discovery all your own,
marveling at the way it invades
the bloodstream, ambushes sleep.

Still, you forgive
so easily. I'd like
to take your young man
by his curls and tear
them out,
who like a dark planet circles
your bright universe

still furnished with curtains
you embroidered yourself,
an underbrush
of books and scarves,
a door at which
you'll soon be poised
to leave.

LOST

Edwin Romond

My mother does as the others do
and sits searching the nursing home floor
for what she's lost. I comb her hair,
the teeth moving through strands
white as my father's shirt for church,
the one she'd iron as we waited upstairs
for baths, her sudsy hands, and soft
Irish singing. When I speak now
she stares at me
and taps her wedding ring to silent music
against her wheel chair.

Today the back door's open,
and this dog with a broken leash
wanders in barking, bewildered.
My mother looks as if she just woke up
and calls *Ginger,* our collie's name
from thirty-five years ago, and the frantic dog
stumbles over and lies beside her chair.
My mother pushes her veined hands into his fur,
whispering *Ginger, Ginger,* her wrist ID tinkling
his tags as she rubs his curly head.
I lean over and, in the soft dark of his coat,
my hands meet hers and she squeezes
her fingers around mine. I place my face
into the shampoo fragrance of her thinning hair,
lost enough to love any name she could call me.

FLYING HOME

after a visit to my mother

Alice Friman

What did she ever want
but to clean house, sing
like Pavarotti with a rag?
New slipcovers, face
at the bottom of the silver bowl.
Then suddenly, the magician
drops a handkerchief and her body
wanders, too small for its skin.
Five feet four to five feet
nothing—the great vanishing
into a pair of house slippers.

What good is understanding
the physiology of spinal disks,
how they crumble like temporary cement?
And what does it matter
knowing all that matters is thrift—the body
huddled around its last nickel of heat
banked for that final conversation?

Dumb heart, you suck in an old crib,
wanting only what you always wanted.
Look around. Above the clouds
roars a planeload of crying babies.

THE TIME IS MIDNIGHT

Marjorie Maddox

My dead father hiccups up the stairs,
down the hall, in my daughter's sleep,
startles her waking, startles me,
with those twins of absence/
presence, staccato air studded
where he isn't, where she is. Which
one of us cries "dada" in the half-light
of street lamps, manmade moons
we howl after as time climbs over
to another date? What we hold
is ourselves holding on,
the language of letting go
untongued in our infant mouths.
I am crying. I am crying.
I am cradling the dear voice
of my child's stirring,
the deep past of my childhood weeping,
rocking all midnights to sleep.

DUET FOR ONE VOICE

Linda Pastan

1.

I sit at your side
watching the tides of consciousness
move in and out, watching
the nurses, their caps
like so many white gulls circling
the bed. The window
grows slowly dark,
and light again,
and dark. The clock
tells the same old stories.
Last week you said, Now
you'll have to learn
to sew for yourself.
If the thread is boredom,
the needle is grief.
I sit here learning.

2.

In place of spring
I offer this branch
of forsythia
whose yellow blossoms
I have forced.
You force a smile
in thanks. Outside
it is still cold,
who knows how long
the cold will last?
But underground,
their banners still furled,
whole armies of flowers wait.

I am waiting for you to die,
even as I try to coax you
back to life
with custards and soup
and colored pills I shake
from the bottle like dice,
though their magic
went out of the world
with my surgeon father,
the last magician.
I am waiting
for you to be again
what you always were,
for you to be there whole
for me to run to with this new grief—
your death—the hair grown back
on your skull the way it used to be,
your widow's peak the one sure landmark
on the map of my childhood,
those years when I believed
that medicine and love and being good
could save us all.

4

We escape from our mothers
again and again, young
Houdinis, playing the usual matinees.
First come escape down
the birth canal, our newly carved faces
leading the way like figureheads
on ancient slave ships,
our small hands rowing for life.
Later escape into silence, escape
behind slammed doors,
the flight into marriage.
I thought I was old enough

to sit with you, sharing a book.
But when I look up
from the page, you
have escaped from me.

LETTER POEM

Margaret Robison

Mother, the tree across from me is such
a fire against the sky.
And underneath it, leaves—
the summer shattered overnight to fall.
A month now you've been dead.
What difference does all we never said make now?
A flock of birds flies past the white
church steeple, back again.
The sky behind them is a watercolor in deep gray.
Everything has grown more vivid in this light
and papers rattle restlessly against a fence
like letters left unmailed—
       Dear Mother, what I meant to say was this...
       Dear Mother, don't you know...

LEGACIES

MID-LIFE

Marjorie Buettner

For a long while now,
I have not wanted to feel
the leap and lunge of my heart
pacing toward its next inexplicable beat
or the whine of blood flooding veins.
I have sought, instead,
the solace of a silent heart
assuming the predictable pulse beneath the skin.
I have lived on the edge of the ring
feeling the heat of the fire on my skin
not wanting to go in.
Protected and camouflaged,
I have motioned through my days
nearly invisible,
but recognizing what I have become,
what I have begun.
Perhaps I have given to my children
that vital thread which,
when carried on,
links them to their past
and future. Often now,
I see what was once unlived in me,
flourish in them.
And I have almost grown accustomed to this.
It is as if I have already written my will
and testament, bequeathing to them
what I no longer need. And I have inherited,
in return, the full force of their fledgling arms
around me feeling, not for the last time,
the fast fluttering of their beating heart
like wings, wings.

REBELLION

Dorothy K. Fletcher

my mother sneaked out
night windows to meet
her James Dean lover
long before she met my father
she let cigarettes droop

from pouty lips
and danced wild dances
my grandmother would
forbid and never saw
thank God because Grandmama

already knew the use
of migraines and ruled
the family with her pains
it was amazing since
she too was wild

stole the family's
Model T and crashed it
into a barn—her lover
my grandfather
along for the bumpy ride

he was forbidden fruit
she eloped with him
because there was this
baby coming
if you know what I mean

so why does it shock me
when my daughter's got
a rose tattoo
picks up boys
no sailor would want to know

perhaps because my rebellion
wasn't loud but raged
beneath the surface
in fantastic angers
that even now frighten me

in the night
when I feel the ancestral
monsters near and sense
my daughter sneaking in
smelling of liquor

and wild smoky boys

SUMMER THUNDERSTORM

Mary Scott

I.

Muggy August night, on the front porch
my son and I sit on the bench
we assembled our first summer here.
He snuggles under a yellow quilt
I made when he was a baby.
His gray kitten curls in his lap.
My arm encircles his shoulders
as we watch veins of lightning fracture the sky.
The air is stifling and heavy with impending rain.
No sound except crickets and frogs,
the "For Sale" sign creaking like a rusty gate
someone forgot to close.

II.

In my childhood, thunderstorms broke
the monotony of endless summer days.
No air conditioning, nights were too hot to sleep
and I read novels under a tented sheet with a flashlight.
Sometimes my mother peeked to see if I was still awake
and invited me to play Chinese Checkers or canasta.
Her freckled arms felt firm as bolsters, comforting
as an upholstered chair when she hugged me.

Long after I trudged off to bed, sleepy at last,
I knew she would still be up, fretting
like a sentinel at an imaginary entrance,
fitting pieces into a jigsaw puzzle
until my father came home from work,
the drone of their muffled voices
reassuring as rain drumming the roof

III.

There are no men in these pictures.
What I recollect of my father was his absence,
present only to fall asleep on the sofa during the news.
My son's father is leaving us, but in truth
he was never here, just a man who came and went,
bellowed or sat remote, tuned to the TV set,
one in every room.

Three summers after my mother's death
my son has forgotten his grandmother
but I long for her cavelike embrace
that dispelled most fears but this,
my son and I drifting into the summer night
aimless as a raft.

FUN DAD

Laura Golden Bellotti

You are somehow there in all the old men
who are older than you ever got to be
in the stoop of their shoulders
their slowing gait
their loose-fitting warm-up suits
the careful way they must learn to carry their fragile bodies.

You never had to know what they know
playing tennis recklessly until the end
against your doctor's orders
playing with the rules recklessly
against the backdrop of breadwinner and father knowing best
playing in secret predictably with women half your age
against my lifelong nightmares, my mother's, my sisters.'

You smiled like a boy
fresh to the world
and the world gave in
feeling foolish for taking itself too seriously
in the sunny face of your adolescent spirit
the fun seeker
the golden boy
the one forever fun.

You were as much fun
as your '57 powder blue T-bird
with the tiny ship-like porthole
I peered out when I was ten
to see if my friends were watching in envy
"Don't you wish you were me—with a father who
drives a car like an amusement park ride!"

You were as much fun
as that other car trip

through France when I was twenty
eating every culinary specialty
from every region on the map
oblivious to calories or cost or capacity
faking French phrases
like a movie star
charming the natives
when no one else could.

You were the unexpected fun
for all your sad vacant girlfriends
who'd almost given up
before they found you
with their false lashes and fur coats
gaily earning my disrespect
in the air-conditioned summers
of my thirties.

You were still smiling
when I was a young forty-three
and you lay immobile on your bed
only a few days left
asking me about the fun
that lay ahead of us that day:
"What's up for this afternoon? Got any good videos?
Why don't you go out and have some fun!"

I loved you for it
for the strained sunny smile
for discounting the pain
for chasing down the fun
until the last possible minute
for believing in the power of fun
for keeping me young.

But I wondered then as I always had
Why isn't he thinking about death?
About the end of fun?
About where you go when the ride is over?

And does he know that all these years
I've been wildly chasing the flip side of his fun
yearning for melancholy like a drug
making love to the darkest side of my inheritance?

You were gone before
the fun was over
before I could ask you
if my cherished sadness was
your dark gift to me
your way of teaching me
what we both needed to learn.

FATHER'S DIAGNOSIS: NAMING NAMES

David Chura

I.

Time bomb.
That's how you describe it.

I'd prefer something prettier, gentler:
slash of birch across pinescape,
smudge of copper beech
or green mirror of maples.

But it's your cancer.
You name it.
Time bomb.
Locked away.
Your body,
case for its own
destruction.

II.

I must've known all along
you were a time bomb:
I picked my way through
the minefield of childhood,
awed by your hair-triggered rage.

Now finally with this naming
I understand.
You were always your own ruin,
this small, final fuse set in you
long before I was born.

III.

It's your cancer.
You name it.
Time bomb.
In naming it,
dare it to explode.
All you ask,
no one else taken.
Just you.
Alone.
Clean kill.

IV.

But it never is.
We both know and never say:
I will be the one left
to tweeze the shards of your sadness and rage
as they work their way
up through memory's bruised skin.

Or perhaps at my days' end
I'll have your courage
to name my demise,
to melt those scraps of mourning
into medals worn proudly,
to finally declare myself
soldier, veteran, son,
survivor of our war.

TATTOOS

Michael S. Smith

Fat in faded black,
the couple and their friend
transported their tattoos,
faded rust and purple-blue,
into the diner, their ten-year-old
son in tow but not led by the hand.

He, too, wore black, bright
and new as his fresh tattoos,
and the silver studs on his leather coat
shone like the polished spokes
of their hogs, leaning against the curb.
He, too, swaggered and stomped his boots.

My own tattoos I wear inside,
and my parents' pricks never bled
where anyone could see them;
she and her mother left him
early, so we always ate alone,
but I owe them a similar debt.

MOMENT

Irene Roach

We are quiet,
She sits beside me,
Directing the hair brush
To the hated task,
Brown strands stand out
Beyond squared shoulders,
To where a waist soon will be.
Unformed lips sound the stroke,
Tan arm keeps the pace.
I touch her hand
To make the quarrel less;
But, she is gone from me
To the tiny place where children hide.
She is difficult for me,
For we are too alike.
Faults of mine I wish hidden
Are before me in her, reminding.
She is the me yet to grow,
And, I would spare her the learning.
I wish her full sprung from defect,
Without the scars of growing.
And the pain of helping will be
Greater than the pain of giving birth.

REPLICATION

Elizabeth Notter

The flash surprised him,
washed the details
from his round face, widened

his fringed eyes as they returned
the strobe's spark.
His pink lips formed

a perfect "Oh"
when I snapped the picture.
You had tipped his small chin up

and still he held his head straight
on the narrow stem of his neck
as he balanced your heavy Stetson,

a few damp hairs straggling
under the brim. You, grandfather,
costumed the 2–year-old squirmer,

not seeing your face and habit blended,
the sifting of generations
of strong and gentle men melded

in this child, who is unafraid,
as you are still
despite 50 years' hard lessons,

and like you, astonished
by what can happen
minute to minute.

RECONNAISSANCE

Gay Davidson-Zieiske

From the depth of my blue studies
I am raised by the heat of your gaze.
Yours is a familiar trance.
You are performing reconnaissance.

For this moment, my peach-fuzzed lip,
the curve of my jaw—are not my own.
Perhaps Aunt Elsie, your sister,
peers through my borrowed hazel eyes.

I have seen you, like Solomon, hold a newborn,
naming part by part his debt to kin.
As a child myself, I did not understand
the mystery of your trance, asking "What did I get?"

I thought of slate-like Indian hair that fell,
a creek at floodtime over logjams.
I hoped for at least the Irish skin,
the laughter like a flight of birds.

Surfacing as if from a daze,
you nodded, spoke in measured pace,
as if you were suddenly brought to light:
"Yes. Yes. From the Smith side, the overbite."

NEW TESTAMENT

William Greenway

I'd never be that
way, white-haired and prophetic,
stern as Solomon, with full pockets.
He'd bend over and out would fall
pens. He'd pick them up and his
notebooks would drop, then
the tiny green Bible. He'd
bend to pick them up and out would fall
pens. *Good night alive,* he'd shout,
almost a saint except for
the squatting mimeograph machine
his own pockets
and his son.

And mother liked James Dean, so for years
it was easy: long hair, leather
jackets, guitars, anything
he wasn't. Until things began
to fall. I made sure they were
cigarettes, small airline
liquor bottles, condoms,
switchblades.

Graying, I bent groaning today in the new
asphalt street to tie my
hushpuppy; the ball of ice
cream tilted out, then the ball
point pens, then another ragged
poem. I stood with an empty cone
in the center of the littered black
street and said God
damn him, and tried to mean it.

FATHERBLOOD

Albert DeGenova

How did he teach me
the subtleties of my body
so like his? How did he teach me
to posture so loosely, to gesture
so emphatically, to smirk so
coolly.
How did he do it? He who was always somewhere
else.
It frightens me when I see him
in a photo of myself.
The man I least want to be
guides the way I cross my legs, the way
I press my hands fingertip to fingertip,
the way I raise my eyebrows.
Fatherblood runs through my veins
like a thief in black, like
moonless midnight.
Do I kiss my own kiss?
What else has he taught me that I cannot see
in windowpane reflections?

HANDS LIKE DADDY

Steve Anderson

I must have squirmed that
first day at the agency when
he came to claim me and I
sought comfort in the hard,
callused cradle of his
electrician's hands.

As a child, I was still uneasy
when I'd watch him wash up
for dinner, scrubbing his
leathery fists raw, unbothered
by that day's new set of scrapes
which wept while he dished up
his only boy's plate and I
wondered, "How will I ever
get hands like daddy?"

Growing up conditioned them
some. Yard work and snow
removal helped firm them.
High school football hardened
them a little more. Hunting
and fishing roughened them
up further.

Yet, at college graduation
his sandpaper handshake
crushed the tender palm
where I'd just received a
literature degree. My dangly
pink fingers hung from
his pudgy grip in a fit as
awkward as adoption.

But now, following a summer
when I called him "boss," and
together we dug thousands of
feet of trenches, laid the same
amount of pipe, and pulled spool
after spool of wire, I examine my
hands and finally see a resemblance.

My nicked knuckles, blistered
fingertips and collection of scabs
teach me how feeling like a
strange man's son is a long
laborious task that involves
spilling the blood we don't
have in common, so that it
can dry into some that we do.

LINEAL PRESENT

Joan Marie Wood

for Alfred Woodcock, oceanographer

My father watches milk swirl in his coffee.
He follows the patterns, creamy vortices,
until drinking mixes the liquids. I remember
his delicate attention, the connection
between his fingertips and the cup,
his voice describing what he saw.

It's hard to imagine my father not
alive to the natural world. He explores
with his eyes, with a light touch, and
begins to explain: how seeds sprout, how seaweed
floats, how raindrops form.

Today I adjust the piano bench, sit
concentrated in a world far from whitecaps,
bubbles, salt. I touch the keys,
listen, and just before I play
I feel my father's fingertips within my own.

LETTER TO A YOUNG CHILD

Rasma Haidri

To write a small note
each day of his first-born's life
did not seem too big a task.
My father's small square printing
filled the three-cent postcards.
They are yellowed now.
The blue ball point lines flattened
under strips of cellophane tape
he wrapped them in.

Later, I watched his hands writing.
It may have been someone's address,
a list of errands, or letters home.
The musical Arabic curving backwards
like a path to retrieve dreams. I loved
his nails shining like quarter moons
under clear lacquer polish.
His long fingers moving the pen
delicately, as with reverence
for a living thing.

In the old college notebooks
where his dissertation notes left off,
I wrote: a city newspaper, spy plans,
interviews on Viet Nam, my first
French words: *Bonjour—Jesuis—J'habite—*
a day by day record of my life in
stories, poems, letters to no one
or the world.

Thus the art is handed down
in pens, the love of paper,
the evening hush in a house

where nothing is said, but by the one writing
to the one who has yet to receive.

When you were two,
I bought a large sketchbook
and began to write.
The small pack of my father's postcards
teaches me to promise nothing.
Only to write. And to imagine him
standing in white shirtsleeves,
his script as measured as the pulse
beating at his temples in the late night house.
When he had only us
and all the time in the world.

GOOD STOCK

Mary Scott

When my father the printer
closed shop he liquidated
the presses and equipment,
furniture and fixtures.

But he couldn't bear
to discard the stock of paper
he'd collected over the years,
reams piled on shelves
just for the sheer pleasure
of stacks of color and texture.

He'd always admired fine stock.
Even out to dinner he'd caress
a restaurant's menu, examine it
like a tailor rubs exquisite fabric
between fingers, murmuring.

I lugged home cartons of surplus,
distributed boxes to siblings,
donated stacks to schools and clubs.
Still, paper overflowed closets,
desk drawers and notebooks.

I compose notes and scribble lists
on creamy parchment, deckle-edged.
I send checks in linen envelopes,
Baronial Ivory, so old the glue is gone
and flaps no longer seal.

I'm spending my inheritance
piece by precious piece.

GIFT

Maureen Flannery

My cityborn sons, children of high-
rise forests, street urchins, learners of
Chicago lingo, are trailing sheep
with my dad, herding the
seasoned ewes and newly
docked lambs from red clay buttes
to mountain's lush ready range.
Home for the summer I've sent
my boys, the boys we were not
the boys my father needed
to ranch in his bootsteps
learn stones and animals
build fences and future
hunt with his rifle and ride
at his side. Here in this overpopulated
flatland with my urban guilt
I've stayed, and sent my boys home
for my dad to be to them all I cannot,
to teach them the rituals enacted
every year through the work
of herders, horses, sheep dogs,
sheep, to share his rodeo
circuit tales and ice water
from a mountain creek, the taste
of venison cooked on a wood stove.
These men will ride together
through sage bush and pine
and more than just my memories
are there, more than the injustices
of their gender and shortcomings of mine.
Something of the child I was not
waits at rock creek where they'll
camp and catch trout for dinner.

Something of the parent I wish to be
circles like a hawk over Billy's Flats
where they'll see the beads of the
Indian grave have sewn the ground
with seeds of a culture rich in respect
for the land we came to after them.
Here in the city with my books I must
relax despite my lacking. For all I could
not be, to father and to sons, being
daughter, mother, I gave each one
the other, he would not have known
             without me.

WILDFLOWERS

Bernice Rendrick

You've left one perfect
fuchsia blossom on the table,
the magenta ruffles like the silk
party dresses you love
for high school dances.

In grammar school you'd cut
through fields, follow paths
along vacant lots, drop lunch box
and sweater to pick wildflowers.
Lupine and poppies drooped
from your young hand when
you came in on spring days.
Twirled like a bone vase
your fingers clutched wild radish,
strands of sourgrass,
a purple thistle bloom.

Years later, gifts appear everywhere!
Peruvian lilies under a tree;
orchids, fragile as heirloom cups
arrive on the porch; a begonia
in a new orange hue swings
from a pine branch. Wide-eyed roses open
wider and wider in the crystal vase.

As the years overlap like petals
we celebrate under the guidance
of flowers that fall at completion.
Us, old stems growing tough.
You a flower we planted to leave behind.

TRANSPLANTING PEONIES

Stuart Gravatt

On an October day, cool, misting, I take
my small shovel, head for the bed of peonies
on the hillside by the family home, begin to dig
into the hard recalcitrant soil. My mother's

peonies, planted here by her forty odd
years ago, have outlasted her, buried, planted
in new soil just a month back. The woman
by my side, her grief as great as mine,

carried on a counterpoint of conversation
with my mother for twenty years, knew her
in ways I do not know. She wants me to take
the peonies, helps me place tenderly the first tangle

of tubers into a white plastic bag. I dig
gently, caught in peony paradox—these same roots
with a tough hold in the earth will snap
at the slightest wrong plunge of spade. I curse,

break many, not knowing where they lie
in the dense, ungiving soil. Their leaves, now
yellow brown, hanging on gangling stems, belie
the white glory, edged with red, of their May blooming,

sweet, thick. Slowly, we gather them, leave
the hill, the rumpled soil, carry them to my car
for the trip to the small city garden where
they will reign against an old brick wall,

proclaiming my mother's legacy.

HEIRLOOM

Rasma Haidri

It is early morning when my daughter
stumbles down the hall
making noises like words, or birdsong,
or leftover memory of angel tongue.
She carries my scarf,
the rose colored one with blue cornflowers
she has slept with for three nights.

She finds me sitting in my room,
climbs up and asks: *Can I keep this forever?*
Until I die? And then I will give it to my child,
and when she is a grown-up
she will give it to her child,
and the story goes on. Is that a good idea?

Yes, I say, that is a good idea,
and notice how the chair can hardly hold us,
already her head reaches to my chin.
Then she whispers: *You will always*
be the grandmother of my child.

WHY I WRITE IN TREES

Kelly Cass Falzone

All I know about my mother is
after I was born she took our
purple black placenta
home in a Tupperware two-quart
and stashed it in the freezer near
tight metal ice trays.
Once the April ground thawed enough
to dig a pit in the side yard that gets sun,
she popped out the bruised blood web
and planted it under new maple roots.

This is what we have begun.

When it feels as if that is all I know
I climb up into the rough limbs of my tree,
peel back a strip of bark and touch
sap-sticky green-reedy wood.
Our blood mixed
travels up tree veins, spreads
into stiff leaves that move light,
and slaps out in shadows
words the earth whispers
to roots.

IF FATHERS SPEAK

Russell Clay

My grandfather spoke to birds in their native tongue. His eyes
were flecked with gold, distant as a cold mountain stream,
and I have seen him cooing instructions to pigeons in the barn.
How often he pulled me to his side, wearing that wide-brimmed
brown rain-stained hat, the spotted hands smelling of Prince
Albert,
the old ivory teeth, the parchment face—but he never said a
word.

My father's word is "Lordy." He still remembers the line he
forgot
in the passion play, when he stumbled from the stage in
shame, a Judas
who never finished the eighth grade. When it rains, when the
stock
market falls, at the fall of man or the rising of a yellow jonquil
after Georgia's unexpected snow, he banks fire against the
hearth
of "Lordy" until it all makes sense. Every morning he writes
my mother
a love letter, and all it says is "Lordy."

When my sons were born I hastened them to talk, but it was
years
before I understood the deep and complex patterns that scrub
stones
round and smooth. I'm thinking of the time we climbed deep
into the cleft of a mountain and Benjamin, the fearless
explorer,
found a stream of icy water. Under each rock, a flake or two
of gold.
Under each stone, a flowing word. We did not speak as we
struggled

up the steep bank grasping wild rhododendron roots, the
    stream-voice
shrinking to the whisper I hear in my bones. When we reached
    high ground
Jeremy said the wild birdsong reminded him of
    great-grandfather,
the presence of wings.

If a man can speak the language of birds, grandfather was
    certainly
perched above us in the brim of an oak. If fathers speak, my
    father
noticed the gold dust in our hair, the wet, torn clothes.
Then warning of the ire of mothers and wives, he took us aside
and whispered "Lordy, Lordy" until we were clean as
    unexpected snow.

LAST WILL

Linda Pastan

Children,
when I am ash
read by the light of the fire
that consumes me
this document
whose subject is love.

I want to leave you everything: my life
divided into so many parts
there are enough to go around; the world
from this window: weather and a tree
which bequeaths
all of its leaves each year.

Today the lawyer plans
for your descendants,
telling a story
of generations
that seems to come true
even as he speaks.

My books will fill
your children's shelves,
my small enameled spoons
invade their drawers. It is
the only way I know, so far,
to haunt.

Let me be a guest at my own funeral
and at the reading of my will.
You I'll reward first
for the moments of your births,
those three brief instants
when I understood my life.

But wisdom bends as life does
around the objects it touches.
The only legacy you need was left
by accident long ago:
a secret in the genes.
The rest is small change.

ABOUT THE CONTRIBUTORS

Liz Abrams-Morley's poems have appeared in many journals and anthologies. Her books include the chapbook *Memory Waltz* (1995) and a limited edition art book, *My Cape Cod,* with Meg Kennedy. Forthcoming is her collection *Learning to Calculate the Half Life.* She is poet-in-residence in schools throughout Pennsylvania and teaches college writing.

Steve Anderson's poems have been published widely in the United States, and recently made their first appearance in Asia by way of a Malaysian travel magazine. He divides his time between Minneapolis and a quiet lake in northern Minnesota.

Linda Tanner Ardison, of Fort Smith, Arkansas, has published poetry and fiction in various literary journals, as well as in two anthologies. She received an *Atlantic Monthly* scholarship to the Bread Loaf School of English and a fellowship grant from the Pennsylvania Council on the Arts. She has worked as an instructor in the Writing Center, York College of Pennsylvania, since 1985.

Rebecca Baggett was born in Wilmington, North Carolina and was educated at Salem College. She is the author of *Still Life With Children* (Pudding House Publications, 1996) and has been nominated twice for the Pushcart Prize. She lives with her family in Athens, Georgia.

Barbara C. Behan is a mother and a writer specializing in women's history and new parenthood. Her nonfiction has appeared in *Indian Artist Magazine, History News* and the *Fairbanks Daily News-Miner.*

Laura Golden Bellotti's poetry has appeared in *Poetic Medicine* by John Fox (Tarcher/Putnam) and a variety of literary journals. Her recent chapbook is entitled *Angleno Birch Tree Girl in* *the Land of Glare.* Bellotti is the collaborator, with Dr. Ana Nogales, on *Dr. Ana Nogales' Book of Love, Sex and Relationships: A Guide for Latino Couples* (Broadway Books/Bantam-Double-day-Dell), and co-author, with Laurie Levin, of *You Can't Hurry Love* (Dutton/Penguin) and *Creative Weddings* (Plume/Penguin). She was the editor of the best-selling *Women Who Love Too Much.*

J.B. Bernstein's poetry and fiction have been published in over 100 journals and anthologies including *Kalliope, Negative Capability* and *The Illinois Review.* She is co-editor of *Our Mothers Ourselves: An anthology of writing and art by women and men.* At this time, Bernstein is working on her first novel.

DC Berry's recent book is *Divorce Boxing* (Eastern Washington University Press).

Harold Black's poetry has been published in literary magazines, including *Visions, Jewish Spectator, Slant, Bitterroot, Potomac Review* and *Virginia Magazine.* A number of his plays have been produced by community theaters, and he has published short stories in *Virginia Magazine.* Two more await publication in *Lucid Moon.*

Gary Blankenburg, former editor of the *Maryland Poetry Review,* is the editor of *Electric Press* and the host of its reading series, *Function at the Junction.* He has written several books of poetry including, *The Illustrated Zen Poet, The Heartland, Pulp Poetry* and most recently The *Blue Movie.* Blankenburg, an English teacher, has written extensively on the work of Robert Lowell, John Berryman, W.D. Snodgrass, Sylvia Plath and Anne Sexton.

Gayle Brandeis is a writer and dancer living in Riverside, California. Her work has appeared in numerous magazines and anthologies, and has received several awards, including the 1998 Quality Paperback Book Club / Story Magazine Short Fiction Award and a 1999 grant from the Money for Women / Barbara Deming Memorial Fund.

Richard Broderick's collection of poems, *The Smallest Place,* was recently published by New Rivers Press. His poetry has appeared in *Laurel Review, Prairie Schooner, Greensboro Review* and many other magazines. He co-edits *Great River Review,* Minnesota's oldest literary journal.

Barbara Brent Brower has poems, short stories and essays in many anthologies and literary journals in this country, in Europe and in Australia. Among publications featuring her work are *The Muse Strikes Back* (Story Line Press), *The Leap Years* (Beacon Press) and *GRRRR, A Collection of Poems about Bears* (Arctos Press).

Marjorie Buettner's poetry and book reviews have appeared in numerous publications, including *Artword Quarterly, The Wolf Head Quarterly, North Coast Review, Rag Mag, Minnesota Poetry Calendar, Loonfeather, Modern Haiku, Red Moon Haiku Anthology* and *Frogpond.* She lives in Minneapolis with her husband and three daughters.

Penny Cagan works as a reference librarian in New York City. Her poems have appeared in many journals and anthologies, including *The Muse Strikes Back: A Poetic Response by Women to Men* (Storyline Press) and *What's Become of Eden: Poems of the Family at Century's End* (Slapering Hol Press). Her chapbook, *City Poems,* was published in 1997 by Chatoyant Press.

Deborah Casillas graduated from the University of California at Berkeley and earned a masters degree from the National University of Mexico. She is the associate director of admissions at The College of Santa Fe.

Siv Cedering has written seventeen books of fiction and poetry for children and adults. Half of her books are in English and half are in Swedish. She has created music, visuals and text for several children's television programs and has exhibited her paintings and sculptures in various locations.

Kelly Cherry's recent publications include *The Society of Friends,* stories (University of Missouri Press, 1999) and *Death and Transfiguration,* poems (LSU Press, 1997). She is Eudora Welty Professor of English at the University of Wisconsin in Madison.

David Chura lives in Connecticut. He teaches incarcerated high school students. His essays and poems have appeared in such publications as *The New York Times, The Anthology of New England Writers, Blueline* and *English Journal.*

Russell Clay's work has appeared in *Poem, The Georgia Journal, Georgia Sportsman, Share* and other publications. His chapbooks, *Half-Life Poems* and *From Ghost Through Bone to Man,* were published by West End Poetry Press.

Susan Clayton-Goldner is a graduate of the University of Arizona's Creative Writing Program. Her poems have appeared in literary journals and anthologies, including *Hawaii Pacific Best of a Decade, New Millennium Writings, The Westwind Review, Animals as Teachers and Healers* and *Our Mothers Our Selves.* She has published two novels. Clayton-Goldner lives on an Arabian horse farm in Williams, Oregon and writes to avoid shoveling stalls.

Michael Cleary's poems and essays have appeared widely. A recipient of a Florida Arts Grant in Poetry (1986 and 1999) and a Featured Lecturer for the National Endowment for the Humanities, his collection of poems, *Hometown, USA,* won the 1992 American Book Series Award from San Diego Poets Press and is now in its second printing.

William Dickenson Cohen was raised in Hawaii, attended Occidental College in Los Angeles and now lives in Brooklyn with his wife and two daughters. His poems have appeared in such publications as *Atom Mind, Poetry Motel, Mind in Motion and Mobius.* His work has been nominated for a Pushcart Prize.

Peter Cooley lives in New Orleans where he teaches creative writing at Tulane University. His six books include *The Company of Strangers, The Room Where Summer Ends, Nightseasons, The Van Gogh Notebooks, The Astonished Hours* and *Social Conversations.*

Ginny Lowe Connors teaches English in a Connecticut middle school. Her work has appeared in such publications as *Calyx, English Journal, Earth's Daughters* and *New England Writers Network.*

Sally Croft's work has appeared in *Buckle &, River Oak Review, Bellingham Review, Seneca Review, Red Dancefloor, Spoon River Quarterly,* and *Baybury Review*. She teaches writing at San Francisco State University.

Barbara Crooker has published poems in such magazines as *Yankee, The Christian Science Monitor, Highlights for Children* and *Country Journal*. She has three children; one married, one in college, one in high school; six books (*In the Late Summer Garden,* H&H Press is the latest), and has won three Pennsylvania Council on the Arts Fellowships in Literature.

Brian Daldorf is a Dad With Two Kids, Brenna and Lucy. He teaches in the English Department at the University of Kansas, Lawrence. His new book of poems, *Outcasts,* is being published by Mid-America Press.

Gay Davidson-Zieiske teaches at the University of Wisconsin-Whitewater. Three anthologies of dramatic monologues published by Heinemann Press: *Baseball Monologues, Elvis Monologues* and *On the Road* feature her work. She has edited or co-editied three anthologies of poetry for Lonesome Traveler Publishing Cooperative. Currently she is writing for radio broadcast as a member of the Mind's Eye Radio Collective in Madison, Wisconsin.

Penelope Deakin and her husband have been raising grapes near Lake Erie for almost forty years. She is the mother of two sons and the grandmother of three grandsons and so has long had a compelling interest in the way young males are socialized. She is also an adjunct lecturer in journalism at the State University of New York College at Fredonia.

Mark Defoe's third chapbook, *AIR,* was recently published by Green Tower Press. Professor of English at West Virginia Wesleyan College, his work has appeared in *Paris Review, Poetry, Kenyon Review, Denver Quarterly, Christian Science Monitor, North American Review, Yale Review, Poetry Ireland Review, Sewanee Review, Poetry International* and many other publications.

Albert DeGenova is a copywriter by day, and a poet and blues saxophonist by night. He is half of the performance poetry duo AvantRetro that appears widely in the Chicago area. His first chapbook, *A Tender Spot,* was published by After Hours Press in 1992; a second book, *Baby, Don't Ya Wanna Go,* is to be released soon.

Victor Depta's poems, stories and essays have appeared in many journals. He has also published five books of poems: *The Silence of Blackberries, The Helen Poems, A Doorkeeper in the House, The House, The Creek* and a novel, *Idol & Sanctuary.* He is the publisher of Blair Mountain Press.

Peter Desy has recently retired from the English department of Ohio University. His poems have appeared in journals such as *The Iowa Review, New England Review* and *Willow Review.* Desy is the author of a poetry collection, *Driving from Columbus,* published by Mellen Poetry Press.

Corrine De Winter, twice nominated for the Pushcart Prize, is the author of six collections of poetry and prose, including *Like Eve, Touching the Wound* and *The Half Moon Hotel.* Her poetry, fiction, essays and interviews have appeared worldwide in over 500 publications, including *The New York Quarterly, Imago, Plainsongs, Yankee, Sacred Journey, The Lucid Stone, Modern Poetry, Home Planet News* and *The Writer.* Her work is featured in the much praised collections *Bless the Day* and *Heal Your Soul, Heal the World,* and in *Bedside Prayers.*

Margaret Diorio edited *Icarus, A Poetry Journal* in Baltimore. Her poems appeared in many magazines and anthologies, winning praise from Robert Penn Warren, May Sarton, Anne Tyler and Dorothy Day. She continued writing after contracting Parkinson's Disease in 1994, until her death in 1997. Her last collection was *End of Summer.*

Arlene Eager received her MS degree in 1978, after some 20 years as a stay-at-home mom. She left a career in nonprofit management about two years ago to devote her time to writing and reading poetry. She and her husband Bill have three children and six grandchildren. They live in Smithtown and New York City.

Constance Egemo lives in Ames, Iowa. Her work has been published in many magazines, including *Yankee, The American Scholar, Twin Cities Magazine* and *Iowa Woman.*

Kelly Cass Falzone's poetry has appeared in *Poets On, Cumberland Poetry Review, Journal of Poetry Therapy* and *Amelia* and has been nominated for the Pushcart Prize. Originally from Rochester, New York, Falzone now works as a family therapist in Nashville, Tennessee, where she lives with her true loves: husband Ron and son Rosario.

Maureen Tolman Flannery, author of *Secret of the Rising Up: Poems of Mexico* and *Remembered Into Life,* has just edited her first anthology, *Knowing Stones: Poems of Exotic Places.* Raised on a Wyoming ranch, she lives in Evanston, Illinois with her actor husband Dan and their wonderful children, all of whom provide much poetic raw material.

Dorothy Fletcher, the mother of a grown son and daughter, is a language arts teacher. She is the author of a children's book, *The Week of Dream Horses* (Green Tiger Press) and her poetry has appeared in numerous journals, including *Kalliope, States Street Review, Key West Review, Messages from the Heart* and *The Artful Mind.*

CB Follett's poems have been nominated for five Pushcart Prizes. She's won several literary awards. Her latest collection of poems is *Visible Bones.* Her anthology of bear poems, *GRRRRR* (Arctos Press) is forthcoming.

Alice Friman is professor emerita of English and creative writing at the University of Indianapolis. Published in ten countries and anthologized widely, she's produced seven collections of poetry, including *Inverted Fire* (BkMk Press, 1997). Among her numerous honors are a fellowship from the Indiana Arts Commission, and the 1998 Ezra Pound Poetry Award for her new collection *Zoo* (University of Arkansas Press).

Ginnie Goulet Gavrin has worked as a massage therapist for twenty years. She is currently at work on a novel concerning the

Gulf War Syndrome. Her short stories have appeared in the journals *THEMA* and *Primavera* and her poetry is soon to appear in *The Worcester Review*. She lives in southern New Hampshire with her husband and son.

Gail Ghai teaches English as a Second Language and serves as a Poet-in-Person for the International Poetry Forum. She is the author of three chapbooks of poetry and is presently working on a book length collection entitled *The House of Cyprus Whispers*. Forthcoming poems will appear in *Shenandoah, Tempus* and *Black Dirt.*

Tim Giles is the father of a healthy thirteen-year-old daughter. He is a Ph.D. student in the Department of Rhetoric, Scientific, and Technical Communication at the University of Minnesota. His poems have been published in *Black Buzzard Review, Sport Literate, Slant, The Ogeechee Review* and in other journals. He is currently working on a novel.

Netta Gillespie lives in Urbana, Illinois. Recent poems and prose have appeared in *Spoon River Poetry Review, Karamu,* and *Snowbound.* She is a past recipient of an Illinois Arts Council Literary Award for Poetry.

Tony Gloeggler runs a group home for developmentally disabled men in Brooklyn. His work has appeared in numerous journals; his first chapbook, *One on One,* was published by Pearl Editions in 1999.

Stuart Gravatt received a BA from Randolph-Macon Woman's College and earned an MA in English Literature at the University of Virginia. She is an independent marketing consultant in Richmond, VA. Ms. Gravatt has been writing poetry for ten years and studying with local poets for five years.

William Greenway's sixth collection, *Simmer Dim,* is from the University of Akron Press Poetry Series. He is professor of English at Youngstown State University.

John Grey is an Australian born poet, playwright and musician. His work has been published recently in *Reed, the Louisville Review, American Writing, Poet Lore* and *Willow Springs.*

Richard Hague is Chair of the English Department at Purcell Marian High School in Cincinnati. His poetry books include *Possible Debris* (Cleveland State University Poetry Center, 1988), *Ripening* (Ohio State University Press, 1984) and *A Bestiary* (Pudding House Publications, 1996). His collection *Milltown Natural: Essays And Stories from A Life* (Bottom Dog Press) was a 1997 National Book Award nominee.

Rasma Haidri lives with her husband and two daughters overlooking the ocean at City of Refuge on the Big Island of Hawai'i. She has lived in France and Norway, and spent time in South Asia, her father's homeland. Her recent poems have appeared in *Prairie Schooner, The Lullwater Review, The Wallace Stevens Journal* and *Fine Madness.*

Tom Hansen teaches writing and literature courses at Northern State University in Aberdeen, SD. His poems, essays and reviews have appeared in *The American Scholar, The Christian Science Monitor, The Georgia Review, The Iowa Review, New York Quarterly, The Paris Review, Poetry Northwest, Prairie Schooner, The Sewanee Review* and other publications.

Rob Hardy has been a Stay-at-Home Dad since 1993. He has published poems, essays and short stories, and has been an active volunteer in his church and community. He graduated from Oberlin College and holds a Ph.D. from Brown University.

Robert Hass, weekly columnist on poetry for the *Washington Post,* Poet Laureate and poetry consultant to the Library of Congress (1995–1997) has published many works of poetry, and is also noted for his success as a literary critic and translator. He has won numerous awards, including the National Book Critics Circle Award in criticism (1984) and in poetry (1997).

Krista Hauenstein is a high school English teacher in the Twin Cities and is the editor of the *Minnesota Poetry Calendar.*

Mariah Hegarty is the editor of the *Manzanita Quarterly,* a Northwest journal of poetry and prose. Her poetry has appeared in *Rogue's Gallery* and the *West Wind Review,* in the chapbook *Lightning Comes Next* and the forthcoming *The Moment Poetry Becomes Possible.* She lives with her daughters in Ashland, Oregon.

Barbara Hendryson's poems have appeared in many magazines, including *Alaska Quarterly Review, Southern Poetry Review, Press, Berkeley Poetry Review, The Sun* and others. Among the anthologies which have featured her work are *Cries of the Spirit* (Beacon Press), *Of Frogs and Toads* (Jill Carpenter Books), *Sixteen Voices* (Mariposa Press) and *Out of the Dark* (Queen of Swords Press). When not writing, she grows herbs and other edibles, and designs/creates walking sticks.

David Sten Herrstrom grew up working with braceros (Mexican farm hands) in the dusty apple orchards of Sebastopol, California. He has published two books, including *Jonah's Disappearance,* a sequence of poems with drawings by Jacob Landau (Ambrosia Press, 1990), and has received a Poetry Fellowship from the NJ State Council on the Arts.

Peggy Hong lives in Milwaukee, Wisconsin with her three children and her husband. Her poems have appeared in publications such as *Bamboo Ridge, Asian Pacific American Journal, Mothering* and *Pudding Magazine.* She is the author of a poetry chapbook, *The Sister Who Swallows the Ocean.* Hong works at Woodland Pattern, a literary center and small-press bookstore, and is enrolled in Antioch University's MFA Program.

Stefan Kiesbye is a student in the M.F.A. program at the University of Michigan. He lives in Ann Arbor with his wife Sanaz.

Galway Kinnell is a former MacArthur Fellow and has been State Poet of Vermont. In 1982 his *Selected Poems* won the Pulitzer Prize and the American Book Award. For some years he has taught at New York University, where he is Erich Maria Remarque Professor of Creative Writing. He lives part of the time in New York City, part of the time in Vermont. His most recent book is *The Essential Rilke,* translated with Hannah Leibmann.

Greg Kosmicki edits The Backwaters Press. His poetry has appeared in *Paris Review, New Letters, Connecticut Review* and others. bradypress published *How Things Happen* in 1997. Missing Spoke Press published *nobody lives here who saw this sky* in 1998. *Marigolds,* from Black Star Press and *tables, chairs, wall, window,* from Sandhills Press are forthcoming.

Norbert Krapf, author of the poetry collections *Somewhere in Southern Indiana* and *Blue-Eyed Grass: Poems of Germany,* directs the C.W. Post Poetry Center of Long Island University. He lives with his wife Katherine and their children Elizabeth and Daniel in Roslyn Heights, Long Island.

Judy Kronenfeld is the author of a collection of poetry, *Shadow of Wings* (Bellflower Press, 1991) and a critical study: *KING LEAR and the Naked Truth: Rethinking the Language of Religion and Existence* (Duke University Press, 1998). She teaches in the Department of Creative Writing, University of California, Riverside.

Jacqueline Kuddler, currently serving on the Board of Directors of the Marin Poetry Center, teaches classes in writing and literature at the College of Marin in Kentfield. Her poems have appeared most recently in *Barnabe Mountain Review, Beside the Sleeping Maiden, Americas Review* and *The Birmingham Review.*

Maxine Kumin, writer of poetry, fiction and children's literature, served as New Hampshire's Poet Laureate (1989–1994), as a consultant for the Library of Congress and a staff member of the prestigious Bread Loaf Writers' Conference. A winner of the Pulitzer Prize, her recent publications include *Connecting the Dots: Poems (Norton, 1996)* and *Selected Poems 1960–1990* (Norton, 1997).

Li-Young Lee, an American Book Award winner, was born in Indonesia and later became an American citizen. He is the author of three poetry collections: *Rose* (BOA Editions, 1986), *The City in Which I Love You* (BOA Editions, 1990) and *The Winged Seed* (Simon and Schuster, 1995).

James P. Lenfestey is a writer based in Minneapolis. His poetry has been published widely around the country and internationally. His journalism and essays have won numerous awards. His book of essays, *The Urban Coyote: Howlings on Family, Community, and the Search for Peace and Quiet,* was published by Nodin Press in 1999.

Lyn Lifshin's most recent book is *Before It's Light,* published in 1999 by Black Sparrow Press, following their publication of *Cold Comfort* in 1997. She has published more than 100 books of poetry, won awards for her nonfiction and edited four anthologies of women's writing including *Tangled Vines, Ariadne's Thread* and *Lips Unsealed.* She is the subject of an award winning documentary film, *Lyn Lifshin: Not Made of Glass.*

Joel Long's book, *Winged Insects,* was chosen by Jane Hirsfield for the White Pine Press Poetry Prize for 1998. His poems have appeared in *Prairie Schooner, Northern Lights, Sonora Review, Poem, Midwest Quarterly, Mothering,* and *Chattahoochie Review, Wisconsin Review,* and other publications.

Candace Love is a Visiting Professor of English at Tougaloo College in Tougaloo, Mississippi for the 1999–2000 school year. Her work has placed in poetry contests sponsored by the College Language Association. She is currently at work on two poetry collections that center on socio-political events and inequities as well as historical reinterpretations.

Naomi Ruth Lowinsky has published poems most recently in *DAYbreak, American Writing, Sow's Ear, Shiela-na-gig, Crab Creek Review* and *convolvlus.* Her first collection of poems, *red clay is talking,* is forthcoming from Scarlet Tanager Books. Her book on mothers and daughters, *The Motherline: Every Woman's Journey to Find Her Female Roots,* was published by Putnam in 1992.

Carol Wade Lundberg teaches creative and technical writing at Santa Rosa Junior College in California. Her poetry and short stories have appeared in numerous journals. Her first book of poetry, *The Secret Life* (Mellen Poetry Press), appeared in 1993. A second book of poetry, *Heresies of Love* will be published this year.

Marjorie Maddox, an associate professor of English at Lock Haven University, has published one full-length book (*Perpendicular as I,* winner of the 1994 Sandstone Poetry Book Award), four chapbooks (*Nightrider to Edinburgh,* Amelia chapbook winner; *How to Fit God into a Poem,* Painted Bride chapbook winner; *Eccelsia,* Franciscan University Press; and *Body Parts,* Anamnesis Press). she lives in Williamsport, Pennsylvania with her family.

Mary Makofske, author of *Eating Nasturtiums* (Flume Press) and *The Disappearance of Gargoyles* (Thorntree Press), has received the Lullwater Prize for Poetry, the Robert Penn Warren Poetry Prize, the *Iowa Woman* Poetry Prize, and the *Spoon River Poetry Review* Prize. She teaches at Orange Country Community College in Middletown, New York.

Freya Manfred is a poet who lives with her husband and twin sons in Shorewood, Minnesota. Her latest book of poetry, *American Roads,* was published by Overlook/Viking, New York. Her memoir, *Frederick Manfred: A Daughter Remembers,* came out in June, 1999 from the Minnesota Historical Society Press.

Tara L. Masih has published fiction, poetry and essays in literary magazines, anthologies and on audiocassette. She has received awards for her work, along with a Pushcart Prize nomination and a finalist grant from the Massachusetts Cultural Council.

Anne McCrady is an east Texas writer and storyteller. Her work has appeared in *Lilliput Review, Midwest Poetry Review, Stoneflower Review, RE:AL, Mediphors, Devo'Zine, 2000 Teas Poetry Calendar, Poetry Society of Texas Book of the Year* and *Rusk County Poetry Society Yearbook.*

Elizabeth McLagan is a free-lance writer, a teacher and a founding editor of *Calyx*. Her poetry chapbook, *The River Sings Like Rock,* was published by Howlett Press in 1990.

Wesley McNair is the recipient of grants from the Rockefeller, Fulbright and Guggenheim Foundations. He has won two NEA Fellowships, the Devins Award, the Hale Medal and prizes in poetry from *Poetry, Poetry Northwest* and *Yankee* magazines. The most recent of his five books is *Talking in the Dark* (Godine, 1998).

MaryLee McNeal writes both poetry and fiction. She teaches poetry workshops for California Poets in the Schools in the San Francisco Bay Area. Her fiction and poems have been published in various journals and anthologies, and her novel, *Home Again,* won the Walter Van Tilberg Clark Award.

Maude G. Meehan is the author of *Washing the Stones, Selected Poems, 1975–1995* (Papier Mache Press). Her work has appeared in anthologies such as *No More Masks* (Feminist Press) *and The Tie That Binds* (Papier-Mache Press).

Angela M. Mendez's poems have appeared in *Twilight Ending, Main Street Raga, Beanfest, Contraband, The Sunday Suitor, Connecticut River Review* and other publications.

Ann E. Michael received a 1998 Pennsylvania Council on the Arts Poetry Fellowship. Her poems and essays have appeared in numerous literary and parenting journals. She lives on seven acres in eastern Pennsylvania with her husband, two children and too many pets.

Wendy Mnookin graduated from Radcliffe College and received her MFA in Writing from Vermont College. Her first book, *Guenever Speaks,* is a cycle of persona poems. *To Get Here,* which contains the poems in this anthology, is published by BOA Editions. In 1999 she received a poetry fellowship from the National Foundation for the Arts.

Judith H. Montgomery is a free-lance editor in Portland, Oregon. Her chapbook, *Passion,* won the 1999 *Defined Providence* chapbook competition. "The White Boat" was co-winner of the 49th Parallel Poetry Prize. She is the mother of two sons, now grown, and has spent her share of time in hospital waiting rooms.

Janell Moon is the author of *The Mouth of Home* (Arctos Press) and *Writing As Spiritual Practice* (soon to be released by Charles E. Tuttle). Diane de Prima says, "Janell Moon's poetry unwraps the mysteries of the ordinary. It is at once familiar, and full of surprises." A longtime San Francisco resident, Moon has a private practice as a hypnotherapist.

Peter Murphy's poems and essays have appeared in *The Atlanta Review, Commonweal, The New York Times, The Shakespeare Quarterly, Witness, World Order, Yellow Silk* and elsewhere. He is a poetry consultant to the Geraldine R. Dodge Foundation and founder/director of the Winter Poetry & Prose Getaway held in Cape May.

Jack Myers has written several books of poetry, including *As Long As You're Happy* (Graywolf Press), winner of the 1986 National Poetry Series, and *Blindsided* (Godine). He is co-editor of the anthologies *New American Poets of the '80s* and *New American Poets of the '90's*, along with Roger Weingarten.

Rochelle Natt reviews poetry for *American Book Review* and *ACM*. Her poetry has appeared in *Iowa Review, California Quarterly, Negative Capability, The Mac Guffin, Fresh Ground, Mudfish, Chachalaca Poetry Review* and in many anthologies.

Bett Notter works for Montgomery County, Maryland's Department of Public Works, where she writes for her cohorts while they fix roads. Her poems have been published in many journals, including *Laurel Review* and *South Dakota Review,* and were among winners of 1999 poetry contests sponsored by *Antietam Review* and *Negative Capability.*

Naomi Shihab Nye's recent books include *Fuel* (poems), *Habibi* (a novel for teens which has won five "Best Book" awards) and *Lullaby Raft* (a picture book). She has edited five prize-winning anthologies of poetry for young readers, including *This Same Sky, The Tree is Older than You Are,* and *The Space Between Our Footsteps: Poems & Paintings from the Middle East.* She lives in San Antonio, Texas.

Sharon Olds' books are *Satan Says, The Dead and the Living, The Gold Cell, The Father, The Wellspring* and *Blood, Tin, Straw.* She teaches at New York University and helps run the NYU workshop at a state hospital for the severely physically challenged. She is currently the New York State Poet Laureate (1998–2000).

June Owens, originally trained as a classical singer, has written poems, book reviews and nonfiction which have appeared widely in journals such as *Atlanta Review, The Caribbean Writer, Manoa* and in many anthologies. She is the recipient of numerous awards, among them a Prospect Press First Poetry Book Award for her 1999 collection, *TreeLine.* She is also the author of the prize-winning chapbook of Japaniform poems, *Willow Moments.* Her new chapbook is *The Mask of Agamemnon.*

Todd Palmer's first book, *Shadowless Flight,* won the Stevens National Manuscript Competition and was published in 1997. His poetry has also appeared in numerous publications including *English Journal* and *Ideals.* He graduated from the University of Florida in 1984. Palmer, who lives in Port Orange, Florida with his wife and three daughters, teaches English at Spruce Creek High School.

Dixie Partridge's poetry and essays are published widely in journals and anthologies. Her two collections are *Deer in the Haystacks* (Ashanta Press, 1984) and *Watermark* (Saturday Press, 1991). She grew up in Wyoming and currently edits poetry for two journals. She and her husband, Jerry, have raised their family of six children in Richland, Washington.

Binnie Pasquier's poems have appeared in *Karamu, Thema, Poets On, Xanadu* and other literary journals and anthologies. She loves language and teaches English as a Second Language. She is a board member of The Long Island Poetry Collective.

Linda Pastan's tenth book, *Carnival Evening: New and Selected Poems 1968–1998* (W.W. Norton), was a finalist for the National Book Award. She was the Poet Laureate of Maryland from 1991–1995.

Miriam Pederson lives in Grand Rapids, Michigan, where she is an Associate Professor of English at Aquinas College. Her poetry has been published in several anthologies, journals and small press magazines including *The Third Coast: Contemporary Michigan Poetry, The McGuffin, Passages North, The Book of Birth Poetry,* and others.. Her poems in collaboration with sculpture created by her husband, Ron, are regularly exhibited in area and regional galleries.

Simone Poirier-Bures is the author of *Candyman,* a novel set in her native Nova Scotia; *That Shining Place,* an award-winning memoir of Crete; and *Nicole* (forthcoming), stories and essays about growing up in Nova Scotia. Her work has appeared in numerous journals in the United States, Canada and Australia; and has been included in eight anthologies. She teaches English at Virginia Tech.

Andrea Potos lives in Madison, Wisconsin with her husband and three-year-old daughter Alexandra. Her poems have appeared in many journals and anthologies, including *Claiming the Spirit Within* (Beacon Press) and *I Feel A Little Jumpy Around You* (Simon and Schuster). A chapbook of her poems entitled *The Perfect Day* was published by Parallel Press of University of Wisconsin-Madison.

Constance Pultz has been writing all her life, and has recently completed a novel. She grew up in New York City and now lives happily in Charleston, South Carolina.

William Reichard is a Minneapolis-based poet and fiction writer. His first collection of poetry, *An Alchemy in the Bones,* won a New Rivers press Minnesota Voices Project prize and his novella, *Harmony,* won the 1994 *Evergreen Chronicles* National Novella Competition. He has had work published in many journals and anthologies.

Bernice Rendrick is a senior writer living in Santa Cruz, California. She has poetry upcoming in the *Monteserrat Review, Passages North* and several anthologies. As wife, mother and grandmother, Rendrick finds family a constant source of inspiration for the writer. She participates in readings, radio and television programs in the community.

Elisavietta Ritchie's *Flying Time: Stories & Half-Stories* contains four PEN Syndicated Fiction winners. Her poetry collections include *The Arc of the Storm, Elegy for the Other Woman, Wild Garlic, Raking the Snow, Tightening the Circle Over Eel Country.* Ritchie edited *The Dolphin's Arc: Endangered Creatures of the Sea.* Another book, *Re-inventing the Archives,* is forthcoming.

Irene Roach's work has appeared in nine books of poetry, in regional news columns, national magazines and publications such as *The Tanka Journal* and *Poetry Nippon* (Tokyo, Japan). She has read her tanka and haiku poetry for the Empress Michiko and the Poetry Reading Circle of Tokyo. Roach is completing a collection of thoughts on old age.

James Michael Robbins is the editor of the *Sulphur River Literary Review* in Austin, Texas. His poetry and short fiction have appeared in various publications across the United States, and in England and Hungary.

Margaret Robison's books are *The Naked Bear* (Lynx House Press/Panache Books, 1977), *Red Creek* (Amherst Writers and Artists, 1993) and *Stroke* (Deerfield River Press, 1996). She has published in numerous journals including *Sojourner, Kaleidoscope, Negative Capability, Yankee Magazine* and has been widely anthologized.

John Roderick is Professor of English and Rhetoric at University of Hartford. He has been named New England Poet of the Year by the New England Association of Teachers of English and has been named Professor of the Year for Connecticut by the Carnegie Foundation for the advancement of Teaching and the Council for the Advancement and Support of Education. His poetry has appeared in many journals and anthologies.

Paulette Roeske's recent collection of poems, *Divine Attention,* published by Louisiana State University Press in 1995, won the 1996 Carl Sandburg Book Award for Poetry. Her other collections are *Breathing Under Water* and *The Body Can Ascend No Higher.*

Edwin Romond is the author of two books of poetry, *Home Fire* (1993) and *Macaroons* (1997). He has received poetry fellowships from both the New Jersey and Pennsylvania State Councils on the Arts and an award from the National Endowment for the Arts. His poems have appeared in many national journals including *Poet Lore, English Journal* and *The Sun.*

Jane Butkin Roth's works of fiction, essays and poetry have appeared in *Poet's Market 1999, Pearl, Rattle, Pleiades, Spillway, ArtWord Quarterly, The Journal of Poetry Therapy, Owen Wister Review* and elsewhere. She had a first place poem in the *Blue Mountain Arts Poetry Card Contest 1999.* An Oklahoma City native, Roth lives in Houston with her three children.

Gianna Russo is Artist-in-Residence with Florida's Arts in Education program and teaches creative writing at Blake Magnet School of the Performing, Visual and Communication Arts. She has administered the Florida Suncoast Writers Conference and directed The Writers Voice of the Tampa Metropolitan Area YMCA. Her work has appeared in numerous publications.

Sylvia Forges Ryan's poems have appeared in journals and in anthologies such as *The Unitarian Poets: A Contemporary Survey, Prayers to Protest, Haiku World: An International Poetry Almanac* and *Haiku Moment.* She has served as editor of *Frogpond,* the international journal of the Haiku Society of America. Currently she is working on a book of poetry about her father, who was a prominent anti-Fascist.

Edith Rylander's poems have appeared in numerous magazines and anthologies and in the collection *Dancing Back the Cranes* (North Star Press of St. Cloud). She is also the author of *Rural Routes: Essays on Living in Rural Minnesota* (North Star Press). The subject of her poem "Two A.M. Feeding" is now a father.

Mark Saba's poetry and fiction has appeared in magazines such as *The Connecticut Review, Confrontation, Kentucky Poetry Review* and *South Dakota Review*. His epic narrative poem, *Judith of the Lights,* was an award winner published by the Mellen Poetry Press.

June Billings Safford's poetry has appeared in periodical such as *Christian Science Monitor, English Journal,* and *Kalliope,* as well as in anthologies, including *From Seed Bed to Harvest* and *Passionate Hearts (New World Library, 1996)*. Safford's fiction and nonfiction work has also appeared in various publications. She is the past editor of *Civil Engineering Newsletter* of Montana State University.

John Sanster lives on Lopez Island, Washington. His work has appeared in several publications, including a recent anthology, *What Have You Lost? Poems Selected by Naomi Shihab Nye.* He recently completed a chapbook manuscript of prose poems entitled *Late Ferry.*

Sharon Scholl is a college professor who teaches world cultures, a church organist and a choir director. Widely published in small press poetry journals, she is the creator of a local TV series called *Poetryworks.*

Joanna C. Scott is the author of *Indochina's Refugees: Oral Histories from Laos, Cambodia and Vietnam,* and three novels, *Charlie and the Children,* a Vietnam war story, *Pursuing Pauline,* a sexual farce, and *The Lucky Gourd Shop,* set in South Korea. *New Jerusalem* received the 1998 Capricorn Award for Poetry.

Mary Scott's poems, short stories and articles have appeared in more than 60 periodicals and anthologies. She wrote a weekly poetry column for the *Ventura County Star* for four years. She lives in Ventura, California with her husband, Don, and has a son, George, and stepsons, Zachary and Nathaniel.

Joan I. Siegel's poetry has appeared in *The American Scholar, Yankee, Commonweal, Amicus Journal, Nightsun, New Letters* and other publications. Her poems are anthologized in *Beyond*

Lament and *American Visions,* among others. Siegel received First Prize in the Anna Davidson Rosenberg International Competition (1998). She lives in Blooming Grove, New York with her husband and daughter.

Linda Simone enjoys looking for the extraordinary within the ordinary. Her poetry has appeared in numerous journals including *Black Buzzard Review* and *Westview,* in three anthologies, and in *ZuZu's Petals* on the web. Her children's book, *Moon,* is forthcoming from Richard C. Owen Publishers, Inc. She lives in Eastchester, New York.

Julia Klatt Singer was born in Chicago near Wrigley Field, and raised in North St. Paul, Minnesota, home of the world's largest concrete snowman. Singer currently lives in Minneapolis with her husband Skip, son Maxwell, fish Danger and dog Ella, a block north of the Mary Tyler Moore house.

Floyd Skloot lives in Amity, Oregon. His poetry collections include *Music Appreciation* (University Press of Florida, 1994) and *The Evening Light,* forthcoming from Story Line. His work has appeared in *The Atlantic Monthly, Harper's, Poetry, The Hudson Review, Virginia Quarterly Review, The Sewanee Review* and elsewhere.

Michael S. Smith's poems and stories have appeared in over a hundred journals and anthologies, most recently *The Chattahoochee Review, Writer's Forum, Connecticut River Review, Chiron Review, The Ledge, Passager and Crescent Review.* He still plies the bureaucratic waters of his job as a risk manager for an international agricultural cooperative, but his lifelong dream of full-time writing will soon be realized.

Thomas R. Smith is the author of two collections of poetry, *Keeping the Star* (New Rivers Press) and *Horse of Earth* (Holy Cow! Press). "Admiring My Father" will be included in a new book of poems about family relationships published by Holy Cow! Press.

Robin L. Smith-Johnson has had poems published in various journals, including *Sandscript, Soundings, Voices International,* and *Yankee*. One of her poems appeared in the *Anthology of Magazine Verse and Yearbook of American Poetry, 1986–88*. She lives in Mashpee, Massachusetts with her husband and three sons. She is the librarian at the *Cape Cod Times*.

Anthony Sobin thinks contributors' notes have a lot more to do with po-careers than po-etry and thus he neither reads them nor provides them!

Susan Spilecki teaches writing and literature at Emerson College and Northeastern University. Her poetry has appeared in *Quarterly West, Frontiers* and *Potomac Review,* and has been nominated for the Pushcart Prize. She recently received a grant from the Vogelstein Foundation for a work in progress titled *Body Blues*.

Elizabeth Spires is the author of four collections of poetry: *Globe, Swan's Island, Annonciade,* and *Worldling*. She has also written several books for children, including *The Mouse of Amherst* and *Riddle Road*. She lives in Baltimore, Maryland and teaches at Goucher College, where she holds a Chair for Distinguished Achievement.

B.A. St. Anderews, whose poems appear in *The Paris Review, The New Yorker, Journal of American Medical Association, The Journal of General Internal Medicine* and *The Gettysburg Review,* is Distinguished Professor in the Humanities at SUNY Health Science Center in Syracuse, New York.

David Starkey teaches creative writing at North Central College and is the editor of *Teaching Writing Creatively* (Heinemann-Boynton/Cook) and co-editor of *Smokestacks and Skyscrapers:An Anthology of Chicago Literature* (Loyola). His poetry collections include *Koan Americana, Adventures of the Minor Poet, A Year with Gayle* and *Open Mike Night at the Cabaret Voltaire*.

Laura Stearns lives in San Francisco, where she contracts her writing services to Bay Area corporations. Her published work includes poems, essays, short stories and one play. A recent essay appeared in the *San Francisco Chronicle*. Her work has been featured in magazines, and on buses and other venues.

Judith Strasser is an interviewer and producer for the nationally syndicated public radio program, *To The Best of Our Knowledge*. Her poems have appeared in *Poetry, Prairie Schooner, Nimrod, The Kenyon Review* and other periodicals. She's the mother of two grown sons who live too far away.

Marlaina B. Tanny's poetry has appeared in literary journals throughout the United States and the Caribbean including Poetry *East, Seattle Review, Confrontation, The Caribbean Writer* and *BIM (Literary Journal of Barbados)*. With her family, she has lived and worked in many places, including nine years in Barbados. She is currently at work on a three-dimensional project of environmental weaving and journal excerpts.

Susan Thomas recently won the Editor's Prize from *Spoon River Review*. Her short story collection was a finalist for the 1999 Bakeless Prize. Her work has appeared recently or is forthcoming in *Nimrod, Confrontation, Columbia, RE:AL, Feminist Studies, New Delta Review, Sheila-Na-Gig, Lullwater Review, Northeast Corridor* and *Kalliope*.

Sue Ellen Thompson is the author of *This Body of Silk,* which won the Samuel Morse Prize from Northeastern University Press, and *The Wedding Boat* (Owl Creek Press). She was resident poet at The Frost Place in New Hampshire in 1998 and recently served as visiting writer at Central Connecticut State University.

Rawdon Tomlinson's latest book is *Deep Red* (University Press of Florida), which won the Colorado Book Award for Poetry in 1996. He has recently taught for University of Northern Colorado and Arapahoe Community College. He lives in Denver, Colorado with his wife and three daughters.

Wyatt Townley lives in Kansas. Her first book, *Perfectly Normal* (The Smith) was a finalist for the Yale Series of Younger Poets, and she recently won a Hackney National Literary Award in Poetry. Poems and essays have appeared in magazines ranging from *The Paris Review* to *Newsweek*.

Claudia Van Gerven won the 1997 Angel Fish Press Chapbook Contest for her collection *The Ends of Sunbonnet Sue.* Her work has appeared recently in *Louisiana Review, Sheila-na-gig, Alacran* and *Calyx*.

Marlene S. Veach is a long-standing member of The Federal Poets. Her work often appears in their publication, *The Federal Poet*, Washington, D.C., and also has been published in poetry magazines and anthologies throughout the United States. She has four published books of poems: *Depth Chart, Deer Woods, The Ease of Freedom's Path* and *Gathering Flowers from the Snow.*

Anna Viadero is a writer living in Montague, Massachusetts. Her work has appeared in publications such as *The Berkshire Review* and *Women's Words*. She has also read her work on the Amherst, Massachusetts public radio affiliate, WFCR.

Doyle Wesley Walls is an Associate Professor of English at Pacific University in Oregon. He has published literary criticism, personal essays, short fiction, cartoons, prose satires and poetry. Walls has been nominated four times for a Pushcart Prize and once for a General Electric Foundation Award for Younger Writers.

Thom Ward is an editor for BOA Editions, Ltd. His poetry collection, *Small Boat with Oars of Different Size,* was published by Carnegie Mellon University Press. He lives in Palmyra, New York with his wife, three children, two cottonwood trees, a dog, a cat and a guinea pig.

Connie Wasem teaches creative writing, composition and the teaching of writing at University of Texas, El Paso. Her poems have appeared in several reviews, most recently *Slipstream, The Oval, American Poetry Monthly, CrazyQuilt* and *Border Voices Anthology*. She lives in El Paso with her husband and daughter.

Mary Ann Wehler is assistant to the Director of The Writer's Voice of Metropolitan Detroit. About her, Plain View Press has said, "This poet has the wisdom of the crone and the energy of the new writer." A poem from Wehler's book, *Walking Through Deep Snow,* was nominated for a 1998 Pushcart Award.

Susan Steger Welsh is the author of *Rafting on the Water Table,* a Minnesota Voices Project winner being published by New Rivers Press this spring. She lives with her husband and two children in St. Paul, where she works as a writer.

Crystal Williams is the author of *Kin* (Michigan State University Press). Her work has appeared in journals and anthologies such as *The Madison Review, Icarus, The Red Brick Review, Spectrum, Catch the Fire, Poetry Nation* and is forthcoming in *Beyond the Frontier.* Her nonfiction work has appeared in *Children of the Dream: Growing up Black in America.* A former member of the Nuyorican Slam Team, she continues to perform her work around the country.

Rebekah Wolman heads the middle school at an independent girls' school in San Francisco. She writes sporadically.

Joan Marie Wood grew up in Woods Hole, Massachusetts. After training as an anthropologist, she worked for twelve years in British Columbia and Saskatchewan as a community organizer. She now lives with her husband in Oakland, California, where she leads creative writing workshops. She has two grown sons.

Jeff Worley has published three collections of poetry, *The Only Time There Is* (Mid-List Press), *Natural Selections* (Still Waters Press), and *The Other Heart* (Devil's Millhopper Press). A fourth collection, *A Simple Human Motion,* is forthcoming from Larkspur Press. Worley's poems have appeared in *College English, The Threepenny Review, Poetry Northwest, The Georgia Review, Shenandoah, The Southern Review* and many other publications. He lives in Lexington, Kentucky.

Sondra Zeidenstein's poems have been published in journals and anthologies, and in a chapbook collection entitled *Late Afternoon Woman.* Her first book length collection of poems, *A Detail in that Story* was published in 1998. She is publisher of

Chicory Blue Press, a small literary press, now in its eleventh year, that focuses on writing by women past sixty.

David Zeiger's collection of poetry is entitled *Life on My Breath.* It includes some sixty poems, most having appeared in various periodicals and anthologies. He's been nominated for the Push-cart Prize, has won several awards and read in many venues. He was Professor of English at the Fashion Institute of Technology in New York City.

ACKNOWLEDGMENTS

Liz Abrams-Morley. "Chemotherapy" and "I Sit, Hypnotized by Storm" are published here for the first time by permission of the author.

Steve Anderson. "Hands Like Daddy" first appeared in *North Coast Review* (winter, 1997) and is reprinted by permission of the author.

Linda Tanner Ardison. "Tears for a Daughter" is published here for the first time by permission of the author.

Rebecca Baggett. "My Daughter's Anger" is reprinted from *Still Life With Children* (Pudding House Publications, 1996) by permission of the author. "Teeth," first appeared in *River City* (1991) and is reprinted by permission of the author.

Barbara C. Behan. "Postpartum" is published here for the first time by permission of the author.

Laura Golden Bellotti. "A Higher Loving" and "Fun Dad" are published here for the first time by permission of the author.

J.B. Bernstein. "Live Long, Die Short" first appeared in *Negative Capability* (Vol. xiv: 1&2) and is reprinted by permission of the author.

DC Berry: "Baby" first appeared in *Poetry* (Vol. 146, No.2, 1985). "Idolatry" first appeared in *Confrontation* (No.60, 61, Fall/Winter 1999). Both are reprinted by permission of the author. "Napoleon's Cigar" is published here for the first time by permission of the author.

Harold Black. "Annual Visit" is published here for the first time by permission of the author.

Gary Blankenburg. "First Love Letter" is reprinted from *The Heartland* (Dolphin Moon Press, 1996) by permission of the author.

Gayle Brandeis. "My Son's Foot" is published here for the first time by permission of the author.

Richard Broderick. "The Violin Lesson" is published here for the first time by permission of the author.

Barbara Brent Brower: "Watching Daddy Play Pinochle" is published here for the first time by permission of the author.

Marjorie Buettner. "Mid-Life" is published here for the first time by permission of the author.

Penny Cagan. "Making It in America" first appeared in *The Jewish Spectator* (fall, 1994) and is reprinted by permission of the author.

Deborah Casillas. "Breakfast with my Father" is published here for the first time by permission of the author.

and also appeared in *The Helen Poems* (Ion Books, 1994). It is reprinted by permission of the author.

Peter Desy. "My Father's Picture on the Cover of a Buffalo Bison's Hockey Program for 1934" first appeared in *Poetry East* (summer, 1983) and is reprinted by permission of the author.

Corrine De Winter. "Womb" is reprinted from *Plainsongs* (University of Nebraska Press, 1995) by permission of the author.

Margaret Diorio. "From a Phone Booth," which first appeared in *The Christian Science Monitor* (1980) and later appeared in *End of Summer* (Icarus Books, 1992) is reprinted by permission of David Diorio.

Arlene Eager. "Wedding Dress" is published here for the first time by permission of the author.

Constance Egemo. "The Swimmer" first appeared in *Dreamworks* (Vol. 1, #2) and is reprinted by permission of the author.

Kelly Cass Falzone. "Why I Write in Trees" first appeared in *Poets On: Coping* (winter, 1995) and is reprinted by permission of the author.

Maureen Flannery. "Gift" is published here for the first time by permission of the author.

Dorothy Fletcher. "Rebellion" is published here for the first time by permission of the author.

CB Follett. "Lost and Found," which first appeared in *Encodings* (fall, 1999) and subsequently appeared in *Visible Bones*(Plain View Press) copyright by CB Follett, is reprinted by permission of the author.

Alice Friman, "Flying Home," which first appeared in *Manoa* (summer, 1995) and later in *Zoo* (University of Arkansas Press, 1999) is reprinted by permission of the author.

Ginnie Goulet Gavrin. "Doing Homework with a Learning Disabled Child," and "Screening" are published here for the first time by permission of the author.

Gail Ghai. "The Last Star" is published here for the first time by permission of the author.

Tim Giles. "Sick Child" first appeared in *Osecchee Review* (1993) and is reprinted by permission of the author.

Netta Gillespie. "For Meg, Leaving Home" first appeared in *Poetry View* (1980) and is reprinted by permission of the author.

Tony Gloeggler. "Rock N Roll" is published here for the first time by permission of the author.

Stuart Gravatt. "Transplanting Peonies" is published here for the first time by permission of the author.

William Greenway. "New Testament" is reprinted from *Where We've Been* (Breiten Bush Books, 1987) by permission of the author.

John Grey. "A Balding Father" is published here for the first time by permission of the author.

Miriam Pederson. "Braids" and "Change of Seasons" are published here for the first time by permission of the author.

Simone Poirier-Bures. "Bloodroot" first appeared in *The Kerf* (May, 1997) and is reprinted by permission of the author.

Andrea Potos. "My Daughter's Eyes" and "Newborn Night" " are published here for the first time by permission of the author.

Constance Pultz. "The Son" first appeared in *Negative Capability* (1989) and is reprinted with permission of the author.

William Reichard. "Northern Light" is reprinted from *An Alchemy in the Bones* by William Reichard (New Rivers Press, 1999) by permission of the author. " The Window, Autumn" first appeared in *The Georgia Review* (Fall, 1998), and then in *An Alchemy in the Bones* (New Rivers Press, 1999) and is reprinted by permission of the author.

Bernice Rendrick. "Wildflowers" is published here for the first time by permission of the author

Elisavietta Ritchie. "Why Some Nights I Go to Bed Without Undressing" first appeared in *Full Moon* (1984) and was reprinted in *Empty Window Review, Out of Season* (Amagansett Press, 1993), *Ladies Start Your Engines* (Faber & Faber, 1996), *A Stranger at My Table: Women Writing About Mothering Adolescents* (The Women's Press Ltd., London) and *The Arc of the Storm* (Signal Books, 1998). It appears here by permission of the author.

Irene Roach. "Moment" first appeared in *Maternal Meditations* and is reprinted by permission of the author.

James Michael Robbins. "The Memory of Grace at Mr. Fontayne's Doughnut Shop" first appeared in *The Maverick Press* (November, 1992) and is reprinted by permission of the author.

Margaret Robison. "Climbing the Mountain in Courage" first appeared in *Courage: Poems and Positive Thoughts for Stroke Survivors,* published by the National Stroke Association in 1996 and is reprinted by permission of the author. "Letter Poem" first appeared in *Minnesota Review* (fall, 1987) and is reprinted by permission of the author.

John Roderick. "Rearview Mirror" first appeared in *The Leaflet* (spring, 1988) and is reprinted by permission of the author.

Paulette Roeske. "In Sympathy, My Daughter Sleeps Beside Me" is reprinted by permission of Louisiana State University Press from *Divine Attention,* by Paulette Roeske. Copyright 1995 by Paulette Roeske.

Edwin Romond. "Lost" is published here for the first time by permission of the author.

Jane Butkin Roth. "Cuttings" first appeared in *Journal of Poetry Therapy* (spring, 1997) and is reprinted by permission of the author. "The Artist's Way" first appeared in *Artworld Quarterly* (fall, 1997) and is reprinted by permission of the author.

Gianna Russo: "To My Boy, Asleep" first appeared in *Gryphon* (1988) and is reprinted by permission of the author.

Sylvia Ryan. "Elegy for my Father" is published here for the first time by permission of the author.

349

Jeff Worley. "Christmas in Tucson" first appeared in *American Literary Review* (fall, 1996) and is reprinted by permission of the author.

Sondra Zeidenstein. "The Day After my Son's Birthday" is published here for the first time by permission of the author. "Now Daughter" is reprinted from *The Crimson Edge: Older Women Writing* (Chicory Blue Press, 1997) with the author's permission.

David Zeiger. "A Poem for Jesse" first appeared in *Wordsmith* (1993) and is reprinted with permission of the author.

Index of Contributors